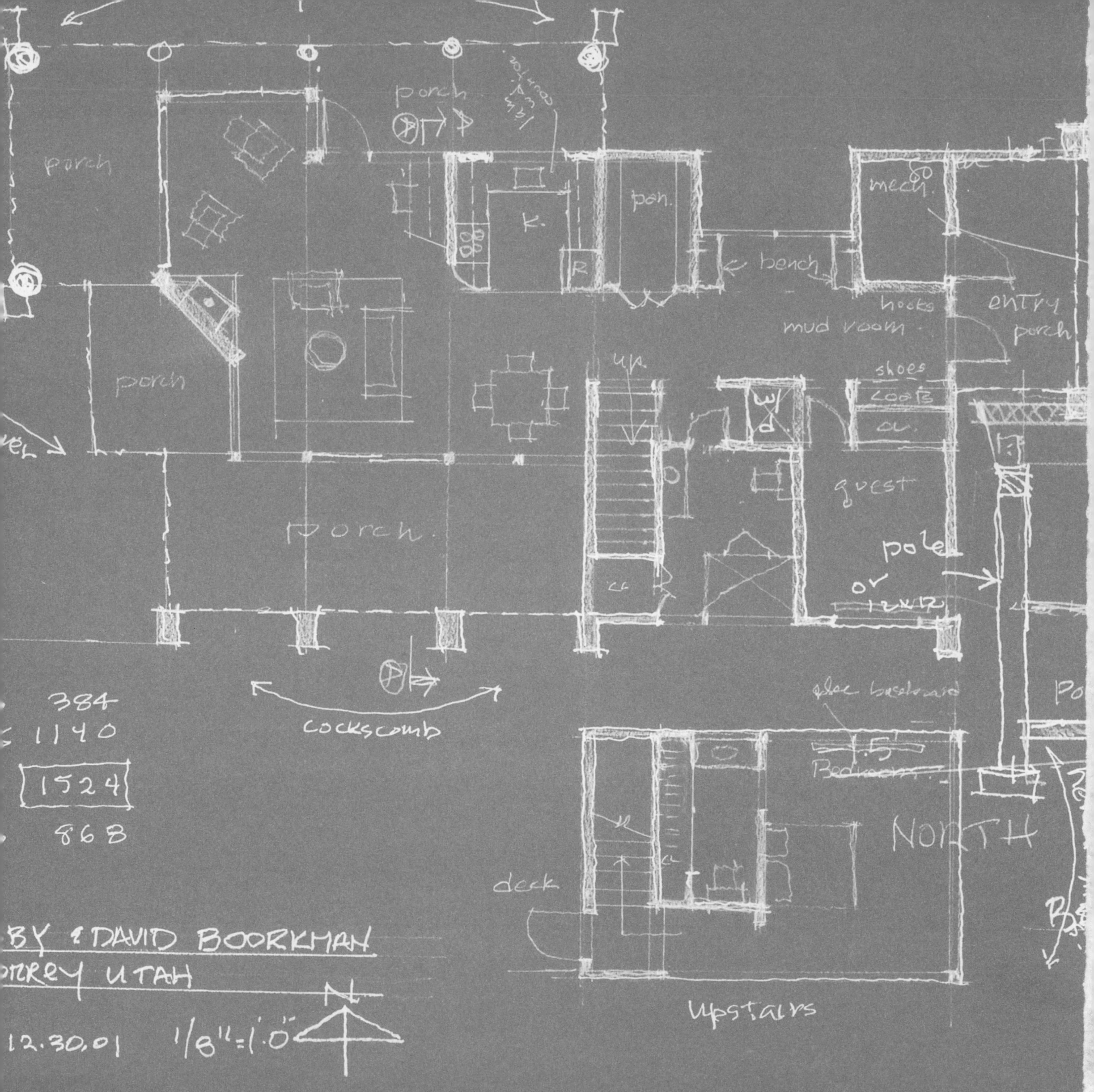
porch
porch
K.
pan.
mech.
bench
hooks
entry porch
mud room
porch
up.
shoes
coats
w/d
guest
porch.
pole or 12x12
cockscomb
384
1140
1524
868
NORTH
deck
upstairs
BY DAVID BOORKMAN
UTAH
12.30.01
1/8"=1'0"
N

DESIGN FOR LIFE

THE ARCHITECTURE OF SIM VAN DER RYN

DESIGN FOR LIFE
THE ARCHITECTURE OF SIM VAN DER RYN

Sim Van der Ryn

Gibbs Smith, Publisher
Salt Lake City

First Edition
09 08 07 06 05 5 4 3 2 1

Published by
Gibbs Smith, Publisher
P.O. Box 667
Layton, Utah 84041

Orders: 1.800.748.5439
www.gibbs-smith.com

Cover designed by Kurt Wahlner
Interior designed by Tom Sieu
Printed and bound in Hong Kong

Library of Congress Cataloging-in-Publication Data
Van der Ryn, Sim.
Design for life : the architecture of Sim Van der Ryn.—1st ed.
p. cm.
Includes bibliographical references and index.
ISBN 1-58685-530-1
1. Van der Ryn, Sim. 2. Architects—United States—Biography.
3. Architecture—Environmental aspects. I. Title.
NA737.V36A2 2005
720'.47'092—dc22

2004030292

contents

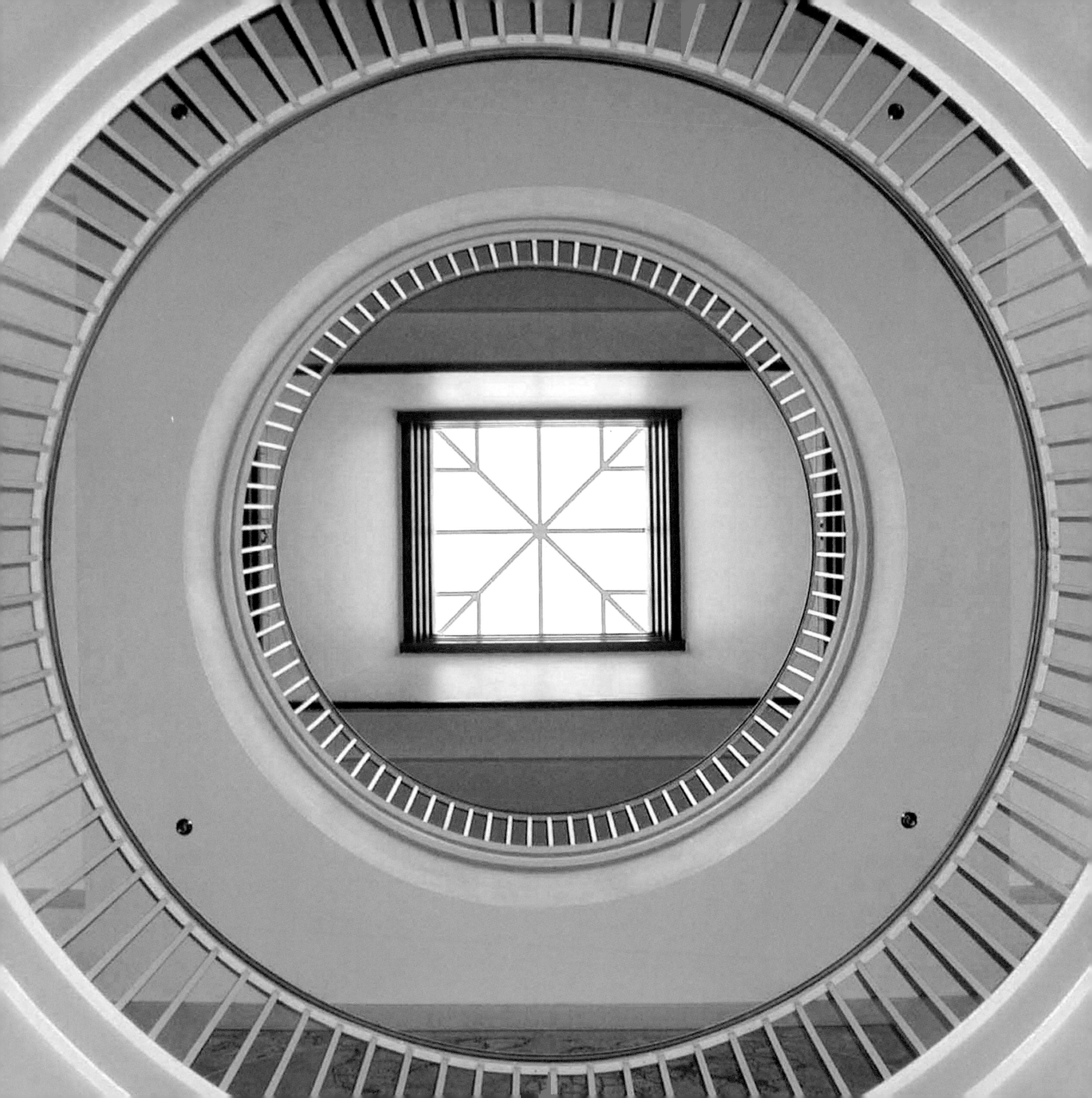

introduction

Where has beauty gone? Since our emergence as a species, humans have been making places and spaces. We've been designing them for the last thirty thousand years. All that practice has made us better at producing more material things, and doing it faster and cheaper. Our advancements in science and technology have provided the knowledge and tools that have allowed us to shape the material world in utterly fantastic ways. But we have lost our ability to create places of beauty, comfort, and durability that fit both the natural world and our own human nature.

Architecture speaks volumes about the culture from which it springs. It is the physical manifestation of values, ideas, hopes, and dreams. Architecture is the human habitat, the environment of our own creation, the skin that separates us from the natural world. It is also a series of walls—physical and mental—that compartmentalize our perception of the world. It doesn't have to be.

Sometime during the last century, architecture lost its soul. Modern culture developed the wealth, power, and technology to create structures that once seemed impossible. While the larger-than-life skyscrapers and the coldly postmodern structures of our time do inspire a detached sense of awe and wonder, very few appear to have qualities that truly move us. Buildings that we truly love are buildings that last. In our modern cities, there are very few that are loved. Beauty and spirit were integral to the works of earlier cultures and times. Today in Bali they still say, "We have no art; we just do everything well."

When was the last time you were moved to tears by a building, or did not want to leave a place because it touched you at such a deep level? When was the last time you shivered, ecstatic, in a man-made place that tugged at something deep inside of you? We travel around the world to experience great works of architecture and cities of the past, but the architecture in which we spend most of our lives leaves us empty.

Our buildings, our suburbs, and most of our cities are cold, lifeless, and disconnected from people. They are uninspiring. To inspire is to breathe life into. How can we make the buildings of our everyday lives fit our deepest human needs? We can design environments that inspire and nourish our souls, bringing architecture into deeper connection with our innermost self.

How can we reconnect buildings and cities to the cycles and flows of the natural world that are the basis for all life on earth? The creation of buildings and the systems that support them—energy, water, waste, roads—is the largest industry in the United States and the industrialized world. This industry is the largest user of energy, materials, and open land, and it is the largest polluter of air, water, and soil. We are still designing and building as though resources are unlimited, without regard to the waste and pollution caused by the construction and operation of buildings and the infrastructure necessary to support them.

LEFT
The Draper Hall renovation at Berea College in Kentucky included a new atrium and skylight for natural daylight and ventilation.

Anyone who is not completely unaware or in denial knows that humans are rapidly changing our planet and our environment in dangerous ways. Our free ride on the back of nature is over. Our children, grandchildren, and future generations face daunting challenges.

Human history is at a critical turning point. Our human capacities for abstract symbolic thinking and testing, the making of ideas and plans as well as material objects and tools, and the ability to turn design ideas into realities have evolved us into unprecedented new worlds and realities. Until recent times, the natural world and its processes were uncontrollable and forced cultures to adapt in order to survive. Now, technology has become the uncontrollable force affecting planetary life support processes and systems such as climate, atmosphere, biologic diversity, and the integrity of planetary biochemical processes such as oxygen production, carbon sequestration, water purification, and soil creation. Technology is rapidly changing the condition of human life support, human culture, and the nature of what it means to be human.

Today no place, no ecology on earth—no matter how remote—is untouched by the consequences of human activities. Most of what we do has unintended and unpredictable chemical, physical, and biological outcomes. More by accident than by design, human civilization controls the conditions of life over the entire biosphere. Fifty years ago, biologist Rachel Carson woke up the world to the law of unintended consequences in *Silent Spring* by connecting the loss of birds and birdsong to the widespread use of the biocide DDT, which produces genetic changes that reduce reproduction in birds. The story has become depressingly familiar as each day additional evidence connects environmental damage to human activities, often through a complex web that connects events far removed in space and time. The growing evidence of damage to basic planetary life support systems brings into question popular views of how humans and nature are connected. No one knows how the story will turn out.

Architecture and urban design can become integrated into the web of life, its cycles and flows. Louis Sullivan, the great nineteenth-century architect, decreed, "Form follows function." I suggest, "Form follows flow."

Buildings are not static objects; they are organisms. Cities are not mechanical assemblies; they are ecosystems. Through ecological design, our buildings and cities can become more fully integrated with nature. Like organisms, they can produce their own energy, and consume and recycle their own wastes without polluting. Design can show us the connection between nature's living cycles and the built environment.

The most advanced science and technology can be used in the service of linking nature and culture more closely together for their mutual benefit. Nature can live without humans, but humans cannot live without nature. Architecture can make this truth transparent and allow us to experience it at a deep, transforming level.

We don't give enough thought to the cost of operating and maintaining poorly designed buildings—a cost that, over the average life span of the building, is four times greater than its initial cost. We don't give enough thought to how to design buildings that can adapt to changing uses, accommodate new technologies, and be dismantled easily so that their components can be reused and recycled. We must begin to think about these consequences.

The mission of green building and sustainable design is to bring architecture and urban planning back to our lives and back to the flows and cycles of nature. We need to reconnect buildings to their roots in climate, land, place, and our human genetic need to be connected to living natural environments. Let's take the pulse of our architecture and lower its metabolism by reducing the obscene, mindless consumption and waste in the name of design. Let's make buildings whole through commonsense design intelligence that incorporates life-enhancing technologies.

Our common work is to shift our dominant worldview from the mechanical clockwork universe of the machine to the intricate, interconnected web-like order that underlies the living world at all scales. What does this shift mean for architecture and design? How can design truly reflect the beauty, intricacy, complexity, and dynamic qualities of the living world?

I have lived the theme implied in the book's title: reconnecting design to people's lives and to living nature. For some years, I have struggled with how to frame a coherent story in words and images that integrates my key experiences, projects, design principles, and philosophy. I had an experience not too long ago that suggested an approach.

Late one afternoon on a wild and wet day, a spectacular double rainbow arched over the bay where I live. I stood on the deck of our houseboat and gazed in awe. I reached for my camera to record the event, but the lens could capture only a small slice of the rainbow. I thought a moment longer and realized that I could take a sequenced series of shots that, when printed and laid out in overlapping sequence, would give a picture of the whole event. I reached for the camera again but when I put it to my eye, the rainbow was gone.

I envision this book like the fleeting rainbow I glimpsed: the outline of a spectrum of ideas and images interrelated in different scales of time and space, both personal and universal.

The separate snapshots form the chapters of this book. The first five chapters cover stories of my life in design and my voyage of discovery and creation: the key events, people, and projects that shaped my ideas and work. I focus on the unfolding process through which the ideas (now labeled sustainable design, ecological design, green architecture, and smart growth) emerged, seeded my imagination, took root through real-time teaching and learning experiments, and grew into architectural and planning projects.

David Brower, the most inspiring environmentalist of our time, challenged modern civilization to "make the ecological U-turn" or face global disaster. The last chapter of this book, "Making the Great Leap Forward," sketches out my thirty-year search to connect the dots between human evolution and its cycles of transformation in relation to the role of design throughout human history.

Our global crisis is also a design crisis as civilization shifts from design processes and products formed in the image of the machine to design based on the forms and processes of the intricately ordered web of life. I lay out the characteristics of the emerging Integral worldview and integral design.

As Gandhi said, "We must be the change we want to see." This is the essence of actively living with hope.

chapter 1

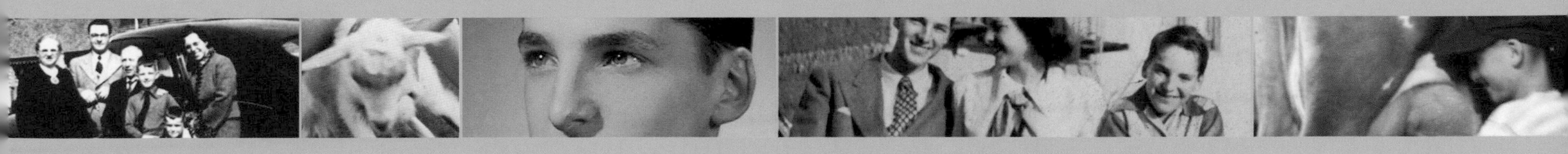

ROOTS AND SEEDS

nurtured by nature

My first memories were made among weeds and puddles, in dusty scraps of nature growing in the nooks and crannies of New York City. I was five years old and this was my refuge, the place where I sought the peace and security I could not find at home.

Home, emotionally, was a place of sharp edges, where I'd prick myself on memories not yet smoothed by time. My family had fled Holland the year before, in 1939, the month the Nazis invaded Poland. My father had feared the Netherlands would be invaded; our hometown, Groningen, was perched in the northeast corner of Holland, perilously close to the German border. We—my parents, older brother, sister, and I—were part of a large Jewish family that had lived in Holland for several hundred years. Leaving was like ripping a tree from the ground. It left roots torn, exposed, and vulnerable.

We replanted ourselves on the outskirts of Queens in a patchwork of six-story brick buildings dotted with marshes and vacant lots. Shaken but resolute, my father tried to arrange exit visas for family members through Cuba and other neutral countries. Our ties were stretched like a tenuous string. For a while we received a thin stream of airmail letters from relatives and friends. The letters grew desperate. Then they stopped altogether. Until the war ended five years later, my parents could only wonder, with leaden thoughts, about the fate of their family and friends. The truth, when it came, crushed any hope that had lingered. Few had survived.

RIGHT
The Van der Ryn family's last days in Holland, 1939. I'm next to my mother on the right.

My parents were unable to share with us their own grief, pain, fear, and worry. They were of a generation that shared little emotion. Their way of coping with the horrors of the time was to lock their emotions inside themselves, to suffer privately under the insulation of daily life. I felt little comfort or warmth at home.

I, too, retreated into my own world, but mine was outside in the green places hidden by ponds and weeds in vacant lots. I found in nature the nurturing I so longed for. I also uncovered my own nature in the search for peace and security that home did not hold. After school I spent every drop of daylight in the patchwork of vacant lots in Queens. I peered, on my hands and knees, at the intricate play of weeds and water, bugs and sun, wrapped up in a kind of dream state. I wasn't looking for anything in particular, just looking. What I found there in that haggard slice of leftover nature was myself.

When you escape one holocaust, you don't want to be part of creating another. Looking back at this time, I see the seeds of my life's work beginning to germinate, grounded immutably in nature and in an innate respect for all living things.

When I had to be indoors, I sought refuge in art. When I was eight years old I went to a drawing and ceramics class taught by a warm German immigrant woman. There I would slip into my dream state, shaping my fantasies into clay or bringing them to life with pencils and paints.

I loved art, but I was happiest outdoors, where I could use my hands and eyes to connect to the teeming natural life around me. I spent summers at camps in the countryside, where nature was everywhere, not just in the cracks. During my high school years, I found summer jobs on farms in New Hampshire and Vermont. There I watched in wonder as sunlight turned into grass and grass turned into cows and cows turned it all into milk. These weren't wild and rugged lands, but places where people lived alongside nature, surrounded by it. This was in marked contrast to the random doses of green I saw in cities.

LEFT
Riding hard on a Dutch goat.

RIGHT
Milking a cow during a high school summer job.

The summer I turned fifteen years old I got my first taste of architecture, though it might be a stretch to call it that. I helped the farm handyman build a Cape Cod cottage from a set of *Popular Mechanics* house plans, which he bought mail order for $9.95. I was fascinated by the process of translating the lines on paper into a three-dimensional space framed with two-by-fours. I learned to love the blistered hands and aching muscles that connected me physically to the structure we built. By the end of the summer, the house had transformed from a sketch to a skeleton to the first draft of a home. The magic of making a drawing into a reality clicked somewhere deep down, a clue to the nature of my calling there in the nexus between art and the world.

Of course, I didn't realize it at the time. As a teenager, I was immersed in the arts. I attended New York City's High School of Music and Art, housed in a 1920s brick Gothic building with a larger-than-life bust of Toscanini in the lobby. The halls rang with a cacophony of sounds from instruments and voices practicing scores. The school was a cultural salad, mixing people of all races and backgrounds. I loved my liberal arts classes—English, history, politics—but I really dove into the fine arts, taking studio courses in drawing, painting, sculpture, and architecture.

LEFT
High school yearbook photograph of the author.

RIGHT
Jack, Fredy, Sim, Heleen, Kew Gardens, 1947.

After the summer spent helping to build a house, I signed up for a high school architecture course. I was drawn to the act of tracing the spaces I created in my mind and building models from those sketches. But to say I had found my calling even then would not be exactly true. As I graduated and started applying to college, I encountered the typical adolescent ambivalence. I wanted to study art, I thought. But my parents, with characteristic Dutch bluntness, asked me, "How will you ever make a living at that?" Architecture seemed a more reliable method of pursuing similar ideals. Without giving it much thought, I applied to architecture school at the University of Michigan. It was the only school I could find that accepted new students in January, when I would be graduating high school.

Just before graduation, I was shipped off to Holland to try my hand at the family business: nonferrous metals distribution. Van der Ryn Metals had been returned to the family after the war, but there was no family left to take it over. My parents and the Dutch managers thought I was a likely candidate. Seeing my family name above a handsome building across from the Queen's palace made me swell with pride and something like ambition, but the gratification I expected from management duties was insufficient for a seventeen-year-old living in Amsterdam. I lasted only a few months.

Not long after, on a freezing January day in 1953, I found myself in Ann Arbor, a freshman at the University of Michigan, living with a gangly, pimply roommate named Arnie. We lived in a cell-like dorm room two blocks from the brick, Gothic architecture school.

It was a letdown. A month earlier, I'd been dizzy with inspiration at graduation, when Eugene Ormandy, the conductor of the New York Symphony, swept us away with the second movement of Brahms's magnificent and somber Second Symphony. With words added, it was our school song: "Now upward in wonder/Our distant glance is turning . . ." Our commencement speaker was Eleanor Roosevelt. Once at the University of Michigan, I missed the incessant hum of creativity that the High School of Music and Art offered, as well as the freedom and intrigue of Holland. Ann Arbor seemed bland, boring, and cold.

The blandness weighed heavily upon me like snow on a flat roof. And it was precisely this flat roof design that unleashed my questioning nature, like an avalanche, upon my unwitting professors.

Architecture school revolves largely around the design studio, where students are given theoretical problems and asked to solve them. The real problem is that the projects are largely contrived instead of practical. And each teacher has a particular set of rules for solving problems the "right" way. I didn't always agree that there was, in fact, a right way.

While an undergraduate, I encountered a few key professors who had been students of Mies Van der Rohe, the German architect who preached the gospel of the flat roof. There we were, in Ann Arbor, Michigan, where snow piles high as houses. It doesn't take an engineer to figure out that snow piles up on flat surfaces, that heaps of snow are heavy, and that roofs are not designed to hold heavy loads. So I designed a building with a pitched roof. The professors were outraged at such temerity! I was always asking Why? and What if? This questioning gained me no popularity with professors, but it stuck with me my whole career.

germinating seeds

At the height of my disgruntlement with architecture school, an epiphany walked in. It came in the form of a short, peripatetic man who we called "Bucky." R. Buckminster Fuller would breeze onto campus and knock us all down with his ideas. He was not a professor, but he spoke frequently on campus, in talks that would start at suppertime and last till three o'clock in the morning. The audience would thin, or snore, as he ranted into the wee hours. But I was awakened. I was struck by his ideas, which sent the pillars of academic theory crashing down like a house of cards.

Bucky, a self-taught engineer whose ideas kept him from sleeping much, visited many architecture schools where he became something of a prophet. He conducted hands-on workshops with friendly faculty, many of whom were his disciples. It might be a cliché to say that Bucky thought "out of the box," but in geometric terms that's pretty accurate. Bucky didn't think in terms of boxes, like so many design professionals of the time. (Flat roofs and boxy rooms were ever present in the modernist architecture of that era.) At the time when I encountered him, Bucky was obsessed with a whole new type of structure that defied traditional architecture and its lexicon. He called the new forms *geodesics.* (Bucky was always inventing new words for new concepts that had no fitting names in the existing language: *synergy, tensegrity,* and *dymaxion* are Bucky words.) The so-called geodesics were spheres, or parts of spheres, made of thin skins stretched like drum hide over slender struts.

These forms seemed alien to the metropolitan eye, but they are common geometries found in nature. You just have to know where to look for them. Geodesics occur at microscopic scales, in marine organisms called diatoms, bug eyes, and molecules (a few of which are named after Bucky).

I remember my first taste of it and how it went to my head like one's first sip of wine. In a first-year class, my classmates and I built a half-dome called a semi-hemi-icosahedron. It was made of diamond-shaped facets, which we made one by one in school wood shop out of lath and timber scraps. The thin diamond frames were covered with a new clear plastic film donated by Dow Chemical. (We now know it as Saran Wrap.) The diamonds looked like kites and were light as a bird's wing. We toted them by the armload to the lawn outside the architecture building, where we pieced them together with thin bolts and wing nuts. In an hour, those unwieldy pieces were knitted together into a beautiful dome shelter that was twenty feet wide and weighed less than a Schwinn bicycle. We sat inside it, munching pizza and drinking beer, surrounded by candles. We could not help but feel wonder at the otherworldly dome, glowing with flickering candlelight in the deepening dusk. Inside, we were glowing too.

Buckminster Fuller's geometries would pop up throughout my career like wildflowers along a winding road. Not long after I built the dome, a fellow student and I teamed up on an assignment to study how these domes showed up in nature. We found them in houseflies' eyes. My friend and I hunted down expensive microphotographic equipment and strong lights to try to capture the forms in images. Through the giant lens we could see the facets of a dome that gave the fly 360-degree vision. The eyes looked like Bucky's domes. Somehow life, form, and function all connected.

Bucky saw the world whole. Through hearing him and making his designs, I began to see the world as whole too. He was a transcendental engineer, a believer that good design could be a tool to solve the world's growing problems through a process he called "comprehensive design science." Though I never had much one-on-one interaction with him—you couldn't interact with him any more than you could with a bolt of lightning—I absorbed his ideas as if he'd been my mentor. Bucky spoke his own language, saying cryptic things like, "There is systematic conceptuality within the totality, but it is always conceptually partial." Bucky was able to see the big picture, how everything was connected. But he also understood the discrete pieces and how they worked. He awakened us to models of good design that were all around us in nature, just waiting to be discovered. He was concerned with reducing waste in manufacturing buildings. He was looking for forms that were inherently strong, that enclosed maximum space for minimum skin area. And every design was an experiment. They didn't always work—the domes tended to leak—but they were the key that unlocked the door to my understanding of the connection between nature and technology.

Even if you know nothing of Buckminster Fuller, you probably know his designs. Many of today's lightweight camping tents are based on his geometries, his ideas about tension and compression. You've probably seen the futuristic ball at Disney's Epcot Center, a giant golf ball without the dimples, towering over Orlando. Its inspiration is clearly Bucky. One of his first large-scale structures was the Ford Rotunda, a geodesic dome originally featured at the 1933 Chicago World's Fair, which was disassembled and reconstructed in Dearborn, Michigan. Once the fifth leading tourist destination in the U.S., the Rotunda was tragically destroyed by a fire in 1962. In 1967, Bucky designed the U.S. exhibit of twenty-story dome housing for the Montreal World's Fair.

Bucky's thinking stretched far beyond structure. Students worked with him to design a mobile unit where one could shower with a pint of recycled water mixed with compressed air. The unit heated its water by tapping the sun and generated electricity with a small windmill. Being a highly mobile individual, he was fascinated with lightweight structures that could be moved. Later, in the 1960s, when many young people were rejecting the boxy icons of industrial culture, they seized Bucky's dome form as a symbol of freedom and mobility. The geodesic dome became an icon for those wanting to invent a new culture.

All these ideas became tools in my own bag of tricks as I began working. For better or for worse, they set me further apart from the dogma of traditional architecture.

After graduating from architecture school and touring in Europe for six months with my new (and pregnant) wife, I found it was time to look for a job. I started in New York. I was interviewed by Gordon Bunshaft, the chief designer of Skidmore, Owings & Merrill. I was impressed by Bunshaft's crystalline design for Lever House, which had just opened. He liked my work. (My Mies-preaching teachers, in spite of my endless questions, had taught me well.) Bunshaft told me to report for work the following Monday.

I filled out all the paperwork and toured the large glass-walled drafting room where the designers worked. There, a hundred men in white shirts and ties bent over their drafting tables. Suddenly I felt I couldn't breathe. I knew my ideas were odd-shaped pegs that could never fit in this square hole. I never showed up for my first day of work. I returned to my parent's brick ranch home in the suburbs and reserved one-way tickets to San Francisco the very next day. It was 1958.

I was drawn west, to the open spaces, wild nature, and spirit of adventure that it represented. I first came out to California with a hometown friend a few years earlier, and I was

"When the student is ready, the master will appear."
—Zen Buddhist proverb

In schools and colleges this wisdom has been turned upside down. Instead of learning by demand according to a student's and a local community's needs, we have learning by command according to the needs of the system. Common sense suggests that significant things are not learned in little pieces at appointed times. If we condition kids over years to accept school learning as the only kind of learning, they will eventually reject other more organic forms of learning.

People learn what they want to learn, when they want to. I used to think my job as a teacher was to be a source of information. After some years, I discovered my job was to help students learn what they want to learn, which often meant discovering for themselves what their values, skills, and intentions were.

hooked. Here, nature swallowed you up. In northern California, the redwoods towered like skyscrapers and the mountains seemed to buttress the impossibly blue dome of the sky. This grandiose, rugged landscape drew me like the moon draws the tides.

After knocking about in several offices, I landed in the firm of Bob Marquis and Claude Stoller. Bob was a squat and bulbous man whose Jewish whine, laced with cigar smoke, preceded him as he moved about the office, chasing trouble. Claude, by contrast, was quiet and earnest. He had worked and taught with Fuller, and now taught architecture at the University of California, Berkeley, in addition to practicing architecture. The small office was housed in an old brick building on San Francisco Bay, right next to the Buena Vista Café, where local legend claims Irish coffee was invented. It was a perfect place to work. Claude was my mentor, while Bob complained that I asked too many questions and was too smart for my own good. "You scare away the customers with all your questions!" Bob chided me. "Why don't you go teach?"

It wasn't bad advice. When a beginning teaching position came up at the University of California, Berkeley, I pounced on the opportunity. The opening required teaching Descriptive Geometry, a course I had neither heard of nor taken. In my interview, the department chair asked, "So, you know all about descriptive geometry, eh?" Of course! I was an expert on the topic. "Good!" he said, "We'll see you in the fall!"

Neither of us knew how much I would learn from teaching.

chapter 2

BRANCHING OUT

"At its boldest, architecture is a statement of an image of living, for the form living takes is the germ of an architecture."

—Rob Straus, former student. *Outlaw Building News,* 1971

The incessant questioning that got me in trouble in my first jobs has driven me to rethink the reasons we do things the way we do—in architecture, in teaching, and in life.

One cornerstone of my philosophy is that every design is a hypothesis. I don't remember if it was Fuller who said it, but he certainly inspired the idea. His projects were all experiments, and they didn't always work. But these experiments tested the hypothetical boundaries of design, and in doing so, expanded those boundaries.

All acts of design are thought experiments if we are conscious of the hypothesis or questions that guide our design. Design always begins with intention, yet seldom are these intentions ever questioned. Moreover, we may not even be conscious of them except in the most basic way. I was always questioning fundamental assumptions, such as the flat roof. I was always wondering: Why? What if? Why do we do things the way we do? The answer is often "Because that's the way it's done." But is that way always the best one? Often not. So how can we approach the problem differently? This is the nature of a thought experiment. It is also the fertile soil in which innovation thrives.

My career has been a string of thought experiments. I tried, with mixed results, to push the boundaries of design, of the rules as I knew them. This chapter surveys thought experiments that were instrumental in my mission to bring architecture back to life. Each one was like a key that opened a door to a new room full of possibilities, leading me into the heart of ecological design, green architecture, and sustainable design.

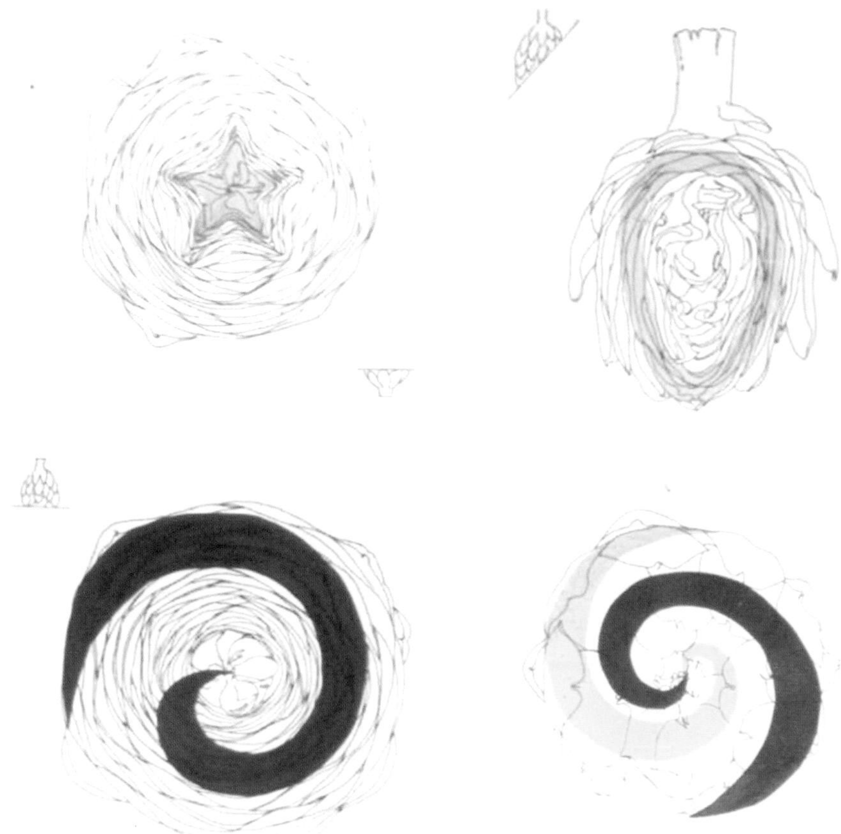

RIGHT
The geometry of artichokes: drawings from UC Berkeley Descriptive Geometry class.

artichokes and geometry
Can I successfully teach what I most want to learn?

In the fall of 1961, the Architecture School at UC Berkeley was housed in a rambling cluster of small rustic buildings covered in redwood shingles, designed by Bernard Maybeck. Everyone fondly called them "the Ark." I held my Descriptive Geometry lectures in the auditorium, where students sat in tiers of ancient Windsor chairs and had their attention spans tempted by a bank of windows opening onto a glorious courtyard.

I would stride briskly to the stage, usually late, and fumble with notes heaped on the small podium. I would stand there, clad in a suit and tie, carving shapes on the blackboard with an eighteen-inch wooden compass and two huge wooden triangles that could well have been weapons. In a flurry of chalk scratching, I'd attempt a profound demonstration of how to render a three-dimensional object in a two-dimension series of points, lines, and planes. What I actually produced was a noble mess and a cloud of chalk dust. I inevitably connected the wrong points or mislabeled a plane. Chalk flew from the end of the wooden compass whipping circles around the chalkboard, and it flew from hissing, laughing students, who hurled it back at me when I made a mistake. Although I had crammed all summer to teach myself the course, and had a cheat sheet clutched in my hand, I didn't know A from A'. I managed to do this for two semesters.

During the next summer I had an epiphany. Actually, it was an artichoke, but it got me thinking. The course, basically, was about how to represent geometric forms in space. The hard part was grappling with all those abstract shapes, those meaningless cubes and planes floating through space. Couldn't I make it more tangible, more interesting? I remembered the enchanting fly's eye microphotographs we'd made in Ann Arbor. I decided to reinvent the course, making it a series of exercises in discovering forms in nature, forms far more profound than cubes and spheres—complex patterns, like those found in artichokes. Good-bye Pythagorean nightmare and chalk!

That year, I strode into class with confidence and a whole new competence. "Your first assignment is to go out and bring me an artichoke," I said. A sea of fresh faces gawked back at me. I instructed them to venture out into nature and look for interesting forms to examine, slice, deconstruct—a tangible, hands-on (and messy) way to discover form. Students returned with armfuls of pomegranates, cauliflower, pinecones, and yes, artichokes. The class had moved into a temporary building left over from World War II. It was a funky but comfortable space with heavy worktables, perfect for a little geometric dissection.

One student plucked the petals of a pinecone and arranged them by size in a spiral with the smallest pieces in the center—a classic logarithmic spiral. Other students cut sections through artichokes and other fruits, discovering intersecting spirals. They photographed, drew, and painted these beautiful geometries, and in doing so, communicated the rules of form they had discovered in the exercise.

I was still teaching Descriptive Geometry but I had shifted the context from a narrow mechanical skill to teaching a way of seeing and discovering form. What my students and I discovered were the basic principles of the architecture of life.

"Education is not the accumulation of information; it is the discovery of essential truth."
—Huston Smith

I heard the scholar of religion, Huston Smith, speak these words at a public lecture. Smith is not a postmodernist, so his conception of "essential truth" is not relativistic and personalized. He is speaking about truths of human existence that are universal and true for all time. Some of these truths are scientific in nature, others are moral, and others have to do with the nature of being human and the nature of nature itself.

I taught a graduate seminar where every week students wrote an essay, "What's true for you," about learning, home, work, money, your body, etc. Their first essays invariably started with "it" and appropriate citations. It took weeks for students to get that the essay "what's true for you" needed to begin with "I." Once this happened there were amazing transformations. I remember a gifted Lebanese émigré student who wrote with incredible passion and detail about the smells of his home in contrast to the olfactory void of our sterile world. As a mature teacher, I saw my job as helping students discover what I called "the architecture of the higher self."

inventing a new field

Post-Occupancy Evaluation

The basic model of architectural design has some surprising parallels to the scientific method. You have a hypothesis (a design), you follow a protocol (design process and construction), and you find out in the lab (the physical world) whether your hypothesis is correct (whether the design works as expected). If it isn't exactly right, as often it isn't, you revise the hypothesis and start over with the next project.

What applied science exists in architecture is limited to its material aspects: structural and mechanical engineering, strength of materials. There is little science with regard to how people and organizations function in built environments. Committees and bureaucracies develop a program of spaces, activities, relationships between them, and qualities they want in a new design. They specify the parameters of time, budget, and performance. Then they turn it over to the architects and contractors, who, when they are done, turn it over to the owners, who fill the building with occupants who use it.

What is missing from this picture? No one does an objective assessment of how the building performs in human terms as a social ecology. Were assumptions concerning how a building would be used correct? What are measures of success? How can they be gauged?

The first several articles I ever had published, one in *Landscape* (Fall 1962) and the other in *AIA Journal* (January 1966), made the argument that architecture wasn't scientific enough in the sense that it failed to articulate hypotheses and test the results. What I was getting at was that architects didn't do any systematic evaluation of whether their buildings worked or not in terms of human ecology, and social and organizational theory.

Huge investments are made in buildings, yet the critical feedback loop that would test whether design assumptions are valid is missing. Instead we rely on a handful of architectural critics who, with increasing infrequency, review finished buildings for a handful of newspapers and professional journals. Committees of peers present awards to what this insular group views as "the best" buildings in their class.

The architectural profession and those interested in architecture are influenced by published reviews of new buildings. Critics review a new work of architecture like they review an art show. Architecture reviewed by a critic based on a visit of a few hours or a day can be disproportionately influential with respect to design trends and the fortunes of individual designers. It's not that such subjective criticism is wrong; it just doesn't add to professional or public understanding of how buildings are actually used every day, how the occupants feel about them, and whether, in fact, they meet the client's stated goals and purposes over time.

My first job in San Francisco was with John Lyon Reid, a respected school architect. We designed mostly windowless schools based on behaviorist research in which a study measured the effect on people of changing a single variable in the environment. In this case, the variable was whether a classroom had windows. An analysis showed that in classrooms with windows, students tended to look out the windows, while in windowless classrooms they looked more at the teacher up front. The conclusion: students "learned better in the windowless classroom, and also learned better if the rooms were intensely lighted and there were no shadows." Thirty-five years later, we have research (by Heschong and Mahone, sponsored by Pacific Gas and Electric) showing that students in schools with daylight get higher test scores than students in classrooms without daylight. (Although the test score indicator may be imperfect, it is much better than the "eyes up front" indicator as a measure of learning.)

The memory of the single-variable, behaviorist, windowless classroom research and the disastrous buildings that resulted from the unthinking acceptance of its findings as science lead me to look for a more multivariable approach to analyzing how buildings are actually used. Establishing how a building is used provides a basis to go back and assess the assumptions that originally determined its form. Environmental analysis has an innovative role to play in the design process by unlocking relationships between form and function that neither client nor architect ever considered.

These types of questions about evaluation of buildings were in my mind when I was a young professor in 1967. I read that the American Institute of Architects had just singled out some new high-rise dorms across the street from the architecture school for an award. The semester was just beginning. It seemed like a perfect project for my seminar: let's find out how the dorms really work for the students living in them. Out of this exercise, we helped invent a new field, post-occupancy evaluation, an attempt to acknowledge that buildings are for people, although most building occupants remain anonymous to the people who commission buildings and to the architects who design them. And as science, post-occupancy evaluation advances a design process that is more rational and more relational with the lived world.

Looking for a project in my graduate seminar, I decided to do an in-depth study of the high-rise dorm complex through participant observation, interviews with occupants, questionnaires, and activity logs kept by residents. We designed these instruments after a lot of initial background research and observations of the buildings at different times of day and night over some weeks, and included informal exchanges with residents. I was interested in developing techniques for multivariable studies that, while they needed some quantifiable indicators, identified clusters of connections between user behavior and spatial design.

At the time, some of the findings were quite surprising:

- The student rooms offered no opportunity for a resident to personalize the space.
- Two students sharing the same room made it difficult to think, read, and study.
- The large common areas meant for social mixing were "as homey as a Greyhound bus depot." The group living rooms felt "like furniture showrooms."
- The corridors became the favorite places for social interaction, with noise and high jinks intruding on the room's private space.
- Houses were the most preferred living arrangement while dorms were the least favored.

Our study suggested that future student housing be designed as low-rise cluster apartments with their own kitchens and living space, rather than as high-rise hotels with centralized common facilities.

Today, the findings of our 1967 study seem self-evident. That is because our work inspired other researchers to evaluate how buildings are actually used, and they came up with some of the same findings.

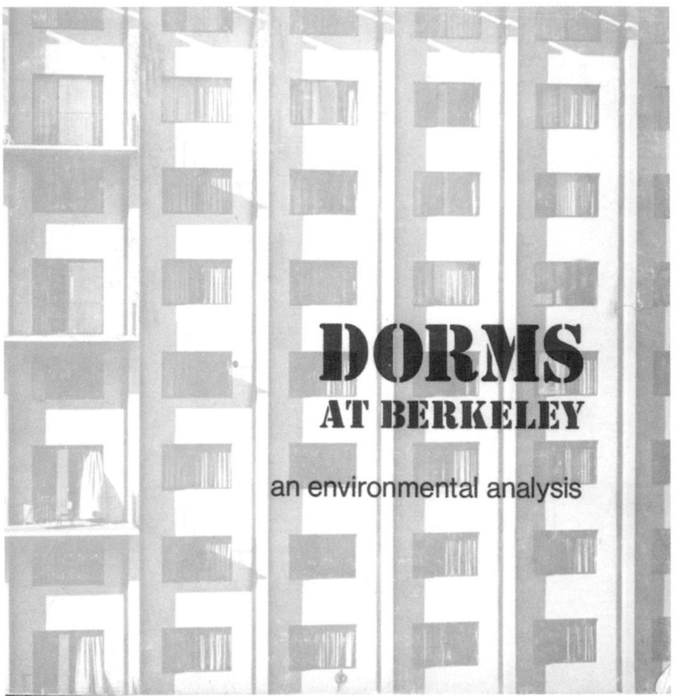

The publication of *Dorms at Berkeley* helped establish the field of post-occupancy evaluation of buildings.

I received a grant from the Educational Facilities Laboratory to write up and publish a report on our dorm research. The resulting 1967 monograph was *Dorms at Berkeley: An Environmental Analysis*, coauthored with Murray Silverstein, one of the participants in the class. Our working title was "The Ecology of Student Housing," based on the idea that a building was not just an object but a living system that included its users; our sponsor rejected the title saying, "No one's heard of building ecology." Our little book changed that.

I remained a loyal, upwardly mobile, young professor who enjoyed the freedom of academic life, adhered in my own fashion to its forms, and appreciated the opportunities the institution had afforded me. So I was surprised when the monograph came out that I suddenly was besieged by requests from student leaders around the country who wanted to distribute large numbers of the book to students. I asked them what purpose they hoped to accomplish. They looked at me in a puzzled, slightly disdainful way. "We thought you wrote this book so student housing would begin to meet student's needs. Who do you think is going to make that happen except students themselves?"

They were stating something that I hadn't considered. In my mind, we had written the book to inform the "expert" class of decision makers: university administrators, those in charge of housing, and architects who designed housing. While an advocate for the users, I never thought the book would be a tool for them to create change. It was a strange disconnect: the schizophrenia of the liberal academic and professional who wants change but rejects the power of direct action by people themselves. *Dorms at Berkeley* was widely read by activist students as well as by the institutional decision makers. Our findings and suggestions did influence future housing policy, and in many places the high-rise hotel concept was replaced by the more flexible and homey apartment cluster.

This first published work on post-occupancy evaluation inspired faculty at Berkeley and other major architecture schools to help create a new field of research about built environments. My colleague Roz Lindheim became a major advocate for changes in hospital design based on similar types of research. Clare Cooper Marcus published a study of a public housing project, which further advanced the field. An architect in New York, Oscar Newman, read my book and went on to write the book *Defensible Space: Crime Prevention through Urban Design,* the first documented attack on the Pruitt-Igoe approach to high-rise public housing. In 1971, a new study area was added to the UC Berkeley architecture curriculum called Social and Behavioral Factors, and a national organization called Environmental Design and Research Association (EDRA) came into being and began having annual conferences. Psychologist Robert Sommer, at UC Davis wrote the book *Personal Space*. Anthropologist Edward T. Hall published *The Hidden Dimension,* regarding personal space and cultural differences in the uses of space. All of this was in the middle 1960s, the beginning of serious social ferment and the questioning of many institutional assumptions, and certainly there was a cadre of architect-researchers who were engaged in this work. The group soon split into two groups: the ones who focused on academic research and the ones who wanted their research to feed directly to the users.

migrant farmworker housing

What does it take to build a village?

In 1964, President Lyndon Johnson pushed through the Economic Opportunity Act (EOA), the centerpiece of the war on poverty. President Johnson was following up on John F. Kennedy's commitment to do something for the vast underclass of the permanent poor in America.

Shortly after the program was funded, my old high school friend Sandy Hirshen and I were visited by Dr. Paul O'Rourke, who had just been appointed by Governor Edmund G. "Pat" Brown to head California's Office of Economic Opportunity (OEO). Paul was an outspoken half-Irish, half-Jewish, Boston-bred physician with a strong social conscience. He had been the Health Director in Imperial County, California's agricultural and political equivalent of the Mississippi Delta, except with migrant Mexican farmworkers instead of former slaves as the exploited class. Paul had come to Sacramento to head OEO after being fired by Imperial County for being too strong an advocate for doing something about the appalling housing, health, and child care situation faced by thousands of migrant farmworkers. Now, full of energy and anger, he was ready to do something statewide.

"What I want you guys to do, is design and build communities for migrant farmworkers in our twenty-two rural counties. I want good temporary housing for families. I want modern health care and child care facilities, and I want it done quickly. Can you have ten camps up and running in six months?" "Of course," we replied, without a clue as to what might be involved. What wasn't involved was bureaucracy. The state OEO had just been set up and we were its first staff and this was its first project. There were no building codes for farm labor housing. How could you write a code for camping under a bridge or sleeping in your battered car, or living in an abandoned shack in which a farmer stuffed as many workers as he could? What was involved was a lot of hostility on the part of rural government and agriculture at state government intervening in a situation the locals took for granted and were uninterested in changing.

Our assignment was not only to design and build the facilities, but also to find sites, which neither local counties nor farmers were eager to provide. The industry needed tens of thousands of workers at harvest time, but they didn't want them living in their backyards. It was a rude introduction to NIMBYism.

We negotiated our first camp site in Linden, a cherry-growing region in the flat Sacramento Delta lands, ninety minutes from Berkeley. We didn't have time to design; we researched tent designs and purchased Paradomes—panelized, twelve-sided tent-like structures invented by a Michigan classmate, Bill Moss, with folding cots and bedding inside. Portable toilets, showers, and cooking facilities completed the camp. It was erected in several days, and a hundred tired, dirty families, many with small children, rushed in like it was the first day of Christmas shopping at the mall. Their smiles and gratitude brought tears to our eyes. Sandy and I drove back to our comfortable homes in Berkeley in silence. We were filled with the mixed emotions of shock and shame at the conditions we had witnessed, and with pride that we had been able to do something, however small, about them.

Setting up an office with a few former students, we began to search in earnest for suitable building systems. My experience with Bucky Fuller served me well, as one of his main interests was lightweight, demountable, low-cost housing systems. As word spread of what we were looking for, backyard inventors of every stripe appeared at our door with their homemade contraptions. Canadian inventor/manufacturer Herb Yates had developed a lightweight emergency shelter made of a new material—foam core—that consisted of two layers of heavy, water-resistant paper bonded to a thin layer of Styrofoam. Each half of the structure was folded into pleats that looked just like a large piece of Japanese origami. The two pleated sides weighed about 150 pounds and, when unfolded, provided the roof and walls for a sixteen-by-twenty-four-foot structure. We designed a lightweight prefabricated floor of plywood and plywood ends with doors and windows, and then mocked up a structure in the architecture school's research lab.

R. Sargent Shriver, President Kennedy's brother-in-law and director of the national War on Poverty program, came to California. Paul O'Rourke had been in touch with Robert Kennedy, who was also developing an interest in what was happening. Shriver appeared on campus with a small entourage, and we showed him our prototype. He was enthusiastic and suggested that I fly back with him to Washington that evening and help design a national program. Not yet a jet-setter, I stammered that my wife and kids were expecting me home for dinner, and I had a class to teach the next day, but thank you anyway!

RIGHT
California migrant worker housing.

LEFT
Sim Van der Ryn (left center) with Dr. Paul O'Rourke (left) and Sargent Shriver (right center), inspecting models of migrant shelter in UC Berkeley's College of Environmental Design Research Lab.

MIDDLE
Prototype of Herb Yates's foam-core housing, set up in the Environmental Design Research Lab.

RIGHT
Migrant family in a *casa acordeona*. We built a number of camps using the folded foam core, which the farm workers called *casas acordeonas* since they unfolded like accordions.

At the same time, Sandy Hirshen worked with manufactured housing companies to develop sturdy, demountable health care and child care center structures. We also had to develop infrastructure for each camp, including electricity, water, and sewage disposal. It was a firsthand realization that community design includes more than designing buildings. Integrating infrastructure was a big part of the whole design problem.

The *casas acordeonas* were novel, but we needed a better solution. We came up with a simple, straightforward answer: we took two sheets of plywood, bonded them to a two-inch-thick slab of Styrofoam, placed a two-by-four at either end, and we had a simple, sturdy building system for walls and roof that required no additional framing. We didn't know it at the time, but we had invented the first structurally integrated panels or SIPS as they are now called and commonly used for high-quality, well-insulated, low-wood-use, prefabricated building.

The plywood panel system became our housing system of choice. Checkerboarded over a utility trench that carried electric, water, and sewage lines, we had a housing system that provided each family with living and sleeping space, bath, and kitchen at a cost of less than $5 per square foot—a $2,000 starter home.

Between 1964 and 1974 Hirshen Van der Ryn designed and executed thirty-three camps to shelter migrant farmworkers and their families throughout the state of California. It was only a temporary solution to a large problem. Emerging farmworker leader Cesar Chavez was more in favor of farmworkers developing their own communities without direct government support, because after an initial period, the California State OEO turned camp management over to county housing authorities who saw the camps as a revenue source and did not share Paul O'Rourke's vision.

I went to Washington in 1967 and in 1968 to brief Robert Kennedy on our program. By then it was clear that his ambitions went beyond the U.S. Senate. During his campaign for the presidency in 1968, he made several swings through the California farm country and was deeply touched by what he witnessed. I believe in his final months he became a changed man, a true champion for social justice. I heard from reporters on the tour that more than once, seeing the conditions under which migrant farmworkers lived and worked in this rich country, Kennedy excused himself to sob silently, away from the cameras.

On the night of June 4, 1968, Sandy Hirshen, Paul O'Rourke, and I gathered together to hear Robert Kennedy's speech from the Ambassador Hotel in Los Angeles. His speech ended, and shortly thereafter he lay dying from an assassin's bullets. Paul, normally quick-talking and articulate, could say nothing. We hugged, no words were exchanged. We each knew that the time that followed would unfold a very different future for our country.

Paper Building and a Bronze Plaque:
A Reflection on Migrant Farm Worker Housing Project

Sandy Hirshen, from *Toward an Architecture of Conscience: The Work of Sandy Hirshen, His Partners and Professional Colleagues.* University of British Columbia School of Architecture Monograph No. 4, 2003.

Our assembled team had a clear sense that we were working at the edge of conventional practice. We were dealing with third-world issues inside a first-world setting. The contrasts were powerful. We had little expectation of having the work acknowledged, but the public had grown aware of the plight of farm workers through the charismatic leadership of Cesar Chavez and the hunger strike he was leading against the grape growers at that time. His unionization efforts had gained national support. The technical innovation of folded foam and paper shelters and the aesthetics of creating a unique tent—only one aspect of our work— quickly came to the attention of the profession. The work was published extensively both in professional journals and the popular press. *Life* magazine ran a full-page photo of the shelter unit.

This was a very heady time for a group of young architects. To receive so much attention for a first professional commission was quite unusual. Someone recommended that we enter this work in the National Honor Awards Program of the American Institute of Architects (AIA). This annual, prestigious competition came with the promise of peer recognition at a national level. In 1968, we submitted our migrant work and the jury panel selected it for an award. Sim, Ralph Gunderson, a key member of our client group, and myself flew to the AIA annual convention in Portland to receive the award.

We assumed that mainstream architecture had embraced these emerging social planning efforts in support of the truly disenfranchised. After the rush provided by the convention in Portland, we quickly settled back into the work at hand. Our office at the time was located in West Berkeley, at 4th and Virginia streets, in an old house with a large side and rear yard, perfect for experimental construction work. It had, in its previous incarnation, been a contractor's office and a storage yard for materials. One afternoon in the fall of 1968, UPS delivered a crate from the AIA offices in Washington, D.C. It was unusually heavy for a package of its size. When I opened the crate, I found, to my surprise, a bronze plaque with appropriate descriptions of the migrant project, dates, and the AIA logo. The AIA had shipped the requisite plaque for winning the award. This was the final installment in the award process.

It is very likely the first time in the history of this particular award that the recognition plaque weighed more than the building it was meant to honor in perpetuity.

people's park: an experiment in collaborative design

Can everyone be a designer?
What are the risks, the necessity of challenging authority?

Berkeley in 1969 was wrapped in the glory of a warm, clear spring. Telegraph Avenue bloomed with the colorful costumes of emergent hippies drawn to the Bay Area scene like flies to butter. The vibrant town buzzed with the bustle of student activity, the thrum of political protests against the war in Vietnam.

Just a block off the postcard-ready Telegraph Avenue lay a festering eyesore—two square blocks of neglected land, a muddy pit of tire ruts brimming with soured spring rain. It was an irritating reminder to the neighborhood of a university plan and process gone wrong. Several years earlier, community residents and the Campus Committee on Housing and Environment, which I chaired, had risen in protest as the University of California, Berkeley, tore down a lovely slice of town to make room for a blockbuster medical center. We might as well have been shouting in the wind. They bulldozed the intricate fabric of old houses and shops that framed one edge of campus. There was no funding for the medical center so they let the land lie fallow. People started using it as a parking lot.

The beginnings of building the People's Park

In a Telegraph Avenue coffee shop, an idea sprang up among a group of locals: Why not turn that vacant lot into a park? Lots of people are showing up in Berkeley, hanging out, sleeping on the street. They need a nice green place to be.

The idea was like a dandelion that scattered its seeds in every direction. A few days later, after coaxing donations from local merchants, a small army self-assembled in the vacant lot, armed with shovels and wheelbarrows. They had no plan whatsoever as they began to dig. Within the following weeks, more and more people joined the effort.

The common cause united folks of all stripes, from students to street people to local residents. It was a magical thing that captured the essence of the time. The battle cry was utterly democratic: "Everybody gets a blister!" Every evening, with aching arms and raw hands, the workers—by this time numbering in the hundreds—would gather around a campfire for an informal potluck and a group meeting to decide on an ever-changing plan.

"Let's dig a pool! That would be cool," someone would say one night. The next morning would see dirt flying from a widening hole. That night, near the edge of the pond-to-be, another voice would tug things in a different direction: "It might be dangerous. Small kids could fall in and drown." Heads would nod and the dirt would go flying right back into the hole. The collaborative design process had no one leader, and so the project seemed to wander with a life of its own. Some might say it was like herding cats. Actually, it was more like getting cats to herd themselves.

Governor Ronald Reagan sprays the Berkeley campus with poison CS gas.

Inevitably some good ideas arose from the mass input, the idea that every voice should be heard because everyone could be a designer. "What about building a central paved court area?" someone said. "I know a place in West Berkeley where they're tearing down a warehouse and there are all kinds of bricks just lying around." This aggregation of information had a way of being simultaneously useful and cumbersome, just like the Internet would later become.

I would often stop by the space that would become known as People's Park on my way home from campus to observe this spontaneous participatory design process. I had just received a grant from the National Institute of Mental Health to document new approaches to design, and this was a case begging to be studied.

Within a few weeks, a park began to take shape. Hundreds of people laid sod, built walls of rubble concrete, laid out paths, crafted crude furniture of found materials, and otherwise shoveled, raked, and bickered. Sweat and sun were the only constants. Each day ended with another open design session where decisions and revisions were made for the following day. There were some people who facilitated discussion and others who had more experience in landscaping and building. But there was no formal plan or organization. This was the grand experiment.

I brought my students to the site to watch like a group of anthropologists and, I admit, to goad folks on. Soon after the dirt started moving, I got a call from Chancellor Roger Heyns. He was fairly new and a bit naïve, having missed the turbulent years of the Free Speech Movement and its aftermath. "What's going on down there on our Durant lot?" he barked. "I hear they call it 'the People's Park.' Don't they know that's University property and they're trespassing?" He was starting to hear from Governor Reagan's office, which assumed these were "outside agitators making trouble."

I politely suggested to the chancellor that he—a psychologist—should visit the site and see for himself. It seemed a positive experiment in community building at a time when the city and the university were floundering in their efforts to relate to an influx of young people in Berkeley. And besides, these "agitators" were cleaning up a blemish of the school's own making. They weren't vandals; they were transforming a nasty, forgotten piece of land into a park built and used by the community. The chancellor replied, "Find out who their leaders are, and call a meeting of your committee. Find a way to get this thing under control!"

His comments acted like water on a grease fire. Posters popped up around town with a photo of a nineteenth-century Native American and a slogan that read "Who Owns This Land?" The text accused the regents of the university of stealing it from the Ohlone Indians, the area's native population. The publicity drew more people than ever to People's Park.

I called a meeting of the Campus Committee of Housing and Environment, and a number of representatives from People's Park showed up. I told them the committee supported their efforts but that we needed to find a way to make it palatable to the university. For example, the College of Environmental Design could take it over as an "Experimental Field Station."

I began to feel a player in a sacrificial dance. More angry words hailed down from Sacramento. The air felt stormy. One evening I took my wife and three grade school kids up to Tilden Park for a school potluck. The children laughed and frolicked, unaware of the trouble brewing. Some talked about the fun they'd had working on building a garden in the park. My heart sank like a stone through their gay chatter. I sensed a no-win confrontation.

That evening, the chancellor called me at home. "You've done your best, but it won't fly," he said. "I'm going to Washington tomorrow morning to chair the Annual Conference of the American Council on Education." He was president of the council.

I protested. "What about you? Can't you take some leadership?" I asked. "Isn't Berkeley an educational institution committed to experimentation and student involvement?" Heyns's reply was cold and blunt. "Look, I'm just a janitor for the regents."

It was mid-May 1969. During the night, a vanguard of National Guard and Highway Patrol seized the People's Park. A crew from San Jose Steel sealed the park with a tall chain-link fence, permitting no one in. The National Guard stood by, dressed in riot gear. Their trappings proved to be a self-fulfilling prophesy.

Daybreak saw chaos and warfare as students and street people rioted, enraged at the stealthy seizure. National Guard helicopters sprayed the campus with a new type of poison gas being tested for use in Vietnam. Alameda County sheriffs armed with shotguns killed one man and wounded others. My kids ran home from school, vomiting and teary-eyed from the poison gas that had wafted into their school.

As the rage and tear gas settled, so did the dream of People's Park. But its ideas spread like a mycelium: threadlike, underground, popping up as mushrooms where conditions are favorable. The ideas and the experience traveled to places far and wide, carried deep in the hearts of the participants. Many, like me, left Berkeley and fled to rural areas free from the controlling hands and eyes of the city. There, people could experiment in designing and building nontraditional homes and communities. I later visited many of these places, where I was inspired by a new type of pioneering: the search for community models that broke free from the cultural norms of 1960s suburban America.

The People's Park experience transformed me in two important ways. Deep down, I felt it was a recapitulation of my family's flight from the impending war in Europe. It shook me to my core, shook me awake. By June, we rented our large home in the Berkeley Hills and moved into a small cabin in Inverness, a wooded ridge on the remote Point Reyes Peninsula. I had built the cabin several years earlier, using the panel system we developed for the migrant farmworkers' housing project. We loaded our possessions in a mail van that barely sputtered up the impossibly steep and winding road and made it to our cabin on the hill.

People's Park
from the book, *People's Park*, edited by Alan Copeland and Nikki Arai, 1969.

It was an incredibly good feeling, building that park. In this country of cement and steel cities, better suited for its machines than for its people, we made a place for people. At a time when only experts and committees, qualified and certified, are permitted to do things, we did something ourselves, and did it well. For all of us, hip and straight, the Park was something tangible that we had done, something that drew our community together. The Park was common ground. People's Park existed for a little more than a month. On "Bloody Thursday," the day the fence went up around People's Park, we took to the streets. The fence stayed up, although the chancellor supported a park, the university professors supported the park, the student body voted for the park, the city council asked for the park, and 30,000 people marched through the streets.

People's Park now stands empty and guarded. The Park died, the idea that created it lives.

Let a thousand parks bloom!

There, in a tangle of nature that was our new home, we were determined to start a new life. We began by building our own home with our own hands. I'd been teaching and practicing architecture for ten years and was ready to expand the building experience I'd had that summer when I was fifteen. The People's Park experience had opened my eyes to the hollowness of conventional institutional forms and their authority. It was time to experiment, to take some risks.

opening up the school box

Toward the end of the 1960s, I began another teaching/learning project with my UC Berkeley students: working with teachers and kids in local elementary schools to redesign their classrooms and playgrounds. This project came together from a number of different directions. It was a time when the schools in Berkeley were just beginning their racial integration efforts. Although the liberal school board and administration weren't admitting it, the sudden clash of two different cultures in the classroom required new approaches to teaching and learning for which teachers weren't prepared.

Soon after the schools were integrated, I decided to visit my children's elementary school just to observe what things were like. I was stopped at the front door by a uniformed guard. "What do you want?" he glowered. "Two of my kids go to school here. I want to see what they're doing." He replied, "They have Parent's Day once a year after school. That's when you're allowed into the school."

I was astonished. My Post-Occupancy Evaluation seminar had migrated from dorms to studying and observing prisons, and here I was at the neighborhood school that had less public access than San Quentin State Prison.

I made an appointment with the superintendent of schools. "I hear you," he politely answered after each of my questions, but he offered no answers. So the next semester I organized a design class that advertised it would work to redesign classroom environments with teachers and students. A book about a British "Free School," called *Summerhill,* was popular. An educational reformer in Berkeley, Herb Kohl, was preaching a similar philosophy. They described a school without a rigid curriculum, where kids interacted and learned within a larger community environment rather than being cooped up in a thirty-by-thirty-foot box for hours a day, sitting at desks bolted to the floor, facing forward.

After networking and finding public school teachers interested in offering their classrooms as guinea pigs for collaborative design and learning experiments, and after making friends with several principals in schools under siege by the unforeseen and unplanned problems of integration, I advertised a design class that would work in Berkeley's elementary schools on freeing up the classroom for learning by doing. Our invitation read:

Dear teacher, no wonder you're tired.
You work nine to three
In a thirty-foot-square box
With thirty kids full of energy.
It's a hard job Squeezing that much energy
Into tiny boxes of space and time.
"It takes a lot of energy
to turn a torrent into a trickle."
George Leonard, "Education and Ecstasy"

Why not make your job easier
And more fun for you and your kids
By opening up your space and time.

One way into learning
Is through learning space —
The classroom, its arrangement,
Its design: what it says about you
And what you do there.

Over the next eighteen months, a group of students formed into a classroom redesign team. Working with teachers and their students, we developed a wide spectrum of ways in which kids could participate in redesigning and re-creating their classrooms using largely salvage materials such as cardboard, carpet samples, fabric scraps, and scrap wood. Kids wanted to supplement the all-pervasive desk with quiet places like library carrels, partitions, resting places,

LEFT Child in classroom with geodesic dome.
MIDDLE Kids' models of geodesic domes
RIGHT 5th graders building a geodesic dome.

and surfaces for pinning papers. We began with simple geometries and gradually evolved more complex geometrical shapes that also taught them about number series, geometry, measurement, and simple building and fabrication skills.

From there we migrated to playgrounds. This was in the days before liability insurance companies dictated equipment design. Working with kids, we designed and assembled a wide variety of structures, mostly using recycled utility poles and rubber tires. This was also in the days before we had a full understanding of the toxins present in these products. We also were entranced with creating inflatable structures, ranging from the ENVIROM, a ring of inflatable vinyl pillows (another chemical no-no of which I wasn't aware at the time), to a room-size inflatable designed and fabricated by our friends, Ant Farm.

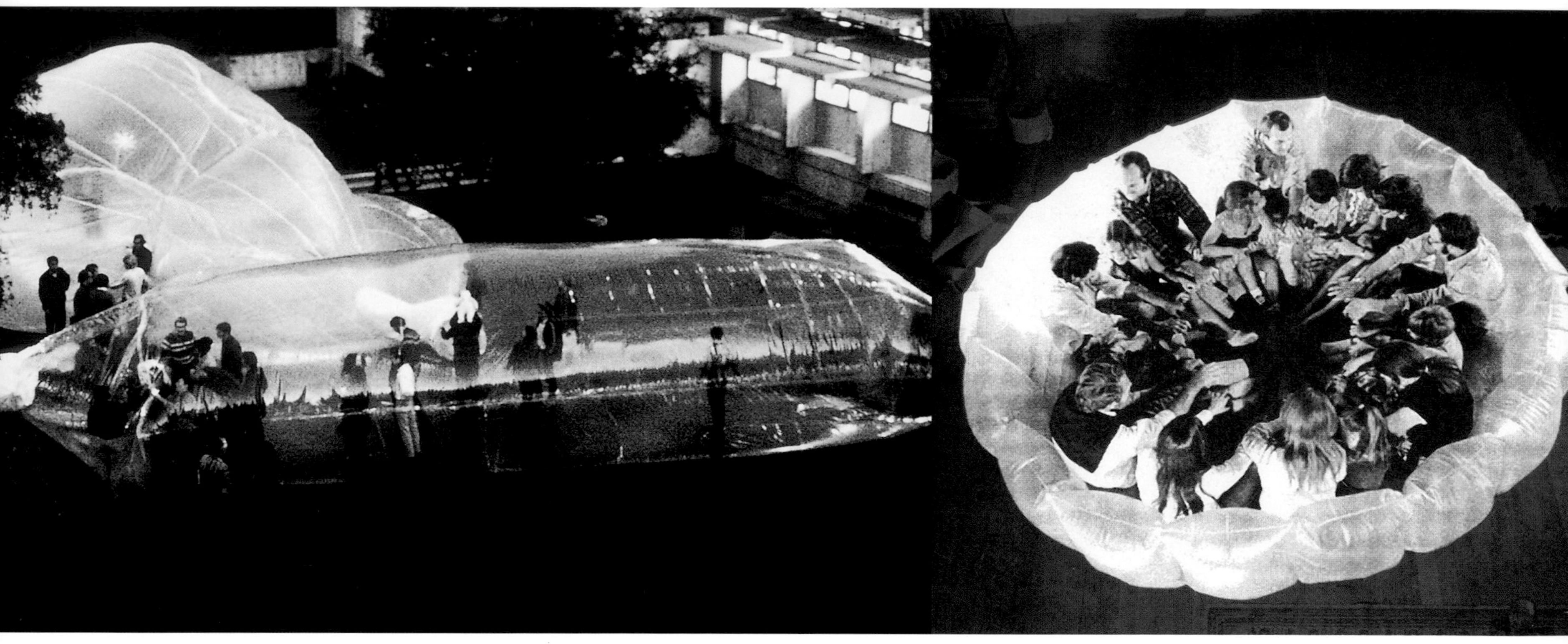

LEFT Inflated plastic environment.
RIGHT ENVIROM, an inflatable group environment.

Jim Campe, a student in the initial class, became the main force for getting things done. We bought a surplus mail van, repainted and named the Eagle, which was outfitted with all the tools and supplies we needed to do one-day makeovers in classrooms. After we moved to the northern California coast in 1969, the group came together to produce a record of our experience, called *Farallones Scrapbook*. The Farallones Islands are craggy outcroppings rising out of the Pacific Ocean twenty-six miles west of the coast. I had named our nonprofit after them because they, the furthest extension of the land called California, are "far out," and you can only see them on the rare clear day when they are not shrouded in fog. We assembled the book on the floor of our new house, printed five thousand copies, and sold them through a newly established independent book distributor called Book People. They soon sold out, and Random House offered to be our copublisher. It was a time when handmade, self-published books chronicling the new West Coast lifestyle were becoming best-sellers. Our book joined that elite circle and our ideas and experiences received a wide readership throughout the country. We had rediscovered the connections between the design of structures and their use by real people.

LEFT Portion of Farallones Designs brochure.
MIDDLE *Farallones Scrapbook* title page.
RIGHT *Farallones Scrapbook,* Micah Van der Ryn's sketch.

chapter 3

FIRST GENERATION ECOLOGICAL DESIGN

Let architecture return to its roots in each person, in each place we make. When people can participate openly and together in making something, then architecture takes on its ancient meaning.

—SIM VAN DER RYN, "Making a Place in the Country"
OUTLAW BUILDING NEWS, SPRING 1972

I spent the summer and fall of 1969 enlarging the cabin on the hill in Inverness into a house. It was my first hands-on building experience since my teenage summer days on a farm and I hadn't gotten much better as a carpenter. I had hired one carpenter to help me. Few people are able to design and build their own home and live in it for most of their lives. The experience has been one of the biggest teachers in my life. Our home has been a continuous work in progress for more than thirty years. The environment surrounding it has lived through years of drought, a major flood, and a forest fire.

Cabin on the Inverness Hill.

making a place in the country

The day we finished the house, I stood up on the road, looked at what we'd built, and had a sick feeling in the pit of my stomach. The cabin had been fine, all six hundred square feet of it, but the house didn't fit the slope. It felt crude and disjointed. The land wasn't suitable for gardening without a lot of terracing. And although there were still only a few houses in this rural subdivision, I knew there were more to come, and this site close to the road wouldn't offer the seclusion we sought.

We found five acres at the end of a steep road that adjoined a six-hundred-acre watershed, which had just been donated to the Nature Conservancy. The five acres were covered with the Bishop pines typical to the entire ridge. *Pinus muricata* reminded me of the pines in Chinese and Japanese paintings with their twisted forms and large crowns (thus the name bishop pine). The land, close to the ridgetop from where we could see the ocean, was largely flat. The closest neighbor was a quarter mile away. Yes, this was the place to build a real home and retreat. The one just finished was a rehearsal.

My former student and colleague Jim Campe and his new wife, Pam, had also moved to Inverness about the time we did. Over the summer of 1971, Jim and I designed a course called "Making a Place in the Country." The idea was to bring a group of Berkeley students onto the five acres I'd just bought and create a living-learning experience where students would collaboratively design and build very rudimentary common facilities: places to meet, cook, eat, bathe, and use toilet facilities. Students would each design and build their own temporary shelter. We'd be designing the social and physical forms for our small, temporary community. We'd also learn from and interact with the local ecology.

I took the idea to Dick Peters, a gentle Southerner who was the chair of the architecture department. Students would spend three days a week on-site and would receive one quarter's credit for the ten-week course. He thought it a fine idea, asking only that when the course was completed we make a presentation of our experiment to the whole school. We advertised the course and chose fifteen applicants, about half men and half women, not all of whom were architecture students.

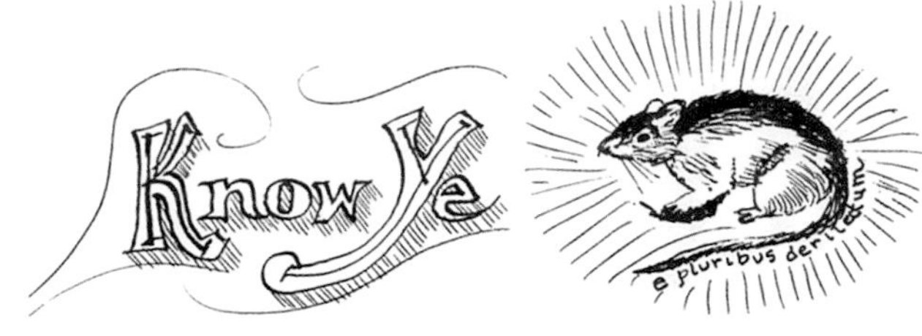

BY THESE PRESENTS: THAT

has made a place in the country
and is entitled to be known to all as
OUTLAW BUILDER
with all the rights and priveleges
attached thereto; December 12, 1971

Sim Van der Ryn — Neotoma fuscipes Rex
James H. Campe — Logistica Maximus

Certificate awarded to Making a Place in the Country class participants. *Neotoma fuscipes* is the Latin name for the native "brown wood rat."

Our first task was to secure some materials. With Jim's 1953 flatbed Chevy truck, Big Red, we went up to Petaluma, a former chicken-raising center, and found Tom King, a former chicken farmer. Tom had helped his dad build coops forty years earlier, before raising chickens was just another high-tech process. For twenty-five dollars each, he sold us ten-by-twenty-foot chicken houses, with floors of old-growth straight-grain fir stained white with decades of chicken droppings and walls and roofs of old-growth redwood gray with age. The class dismantled them, and we had our lumberyard. One student wrote, "You took care taking down what Tom had built so carefully before, feeling good that the coops would not die—but only be transformed."

First things first. We built an old-fashioned outhouse. That done, we tackled building a kitchen out of the recycled coop material. Another student commented, "It seems the group really came together when we raised the chicken coop roof on the kitchen framing. Funny, a little thing like that." Then we began to build a sixteen-by-twenty-four-foot structure that would serve as our meeting place and indoor workspace. We quickly called it "the Ark," after the original Bernard Maybeck–designed, wooden architecture building on the Berkeley campus.

LEFT
Students dismantling a chicken coop.

RIGHT
Jim Campe (above) and Sim Van der Ryn building in Inverness.

When we were laying it out in the woods, it appeared we'd have to remove several young bishop pine trees. Work stopped and the group gathered for what turned into a long emotional discussion of the ethical and practical trade-offs between what humans want and what nature wants. Some in the group felt it wrong to destroy any young trees. I'd gone through a similar internal dialogue in building my first cabin, coming to the conclusion that we were living in a pine forest where young trees were constantly regenerating the forest and not all would survive in the competition for light. We let the discussion run its course, and in the end decided that sacrificing a few young trees did no harm to the forest. It was a valuable lesson in seeing the whole, rather than simply the parts.

As the Ark, the center of our class community, took shape, each student was invited to build their own personal shelter. Paul built a lightweight tree house with a plastic bubble roof high up in an old oak, with incredible views of the bay that stretched out below. Martha built a Japanese-feeling covered platform: "I wanted my own place sunny, quiet, among trees and ferns." Others built intricate structures such as tepees and capsule-like structures suspended with surplus hawser line from sturdy branches. Some made floors from the circular ends of large cable spools. The individual act of imagining and building simple shelter within a community evoked deep feelings.

Everyone was required to keep a daily journal. Here are a few excerpts:

"Perhaps the greatest pleasure was seeing others using and living in places that you helped build."

"I think the most important thing I've learned is that building requires belief in what you are doing, belief that you can do it, belief that it is good."

"Lifting a beam or a roof was always a high (pure positive energy)—energies touched through some shared task. Somehow afterwards it seemed easier to be friends."

"The class instilled not just a fundamental knowledge of building, but a confidence to undertake projects otherwise beyond our realm. Confidence to follow a vision."

"Instead of an inventory of ideas which needed to be filed in separate stacks in my mind, I found that I was constantly taking a stream of concepts and actions which followed a continuous sequence. My individual actions seemed to be part of a group action which followed a course of its own, separate from all the individual ideas."

"How to, how to, how many how to's did I learn these ten weeks, embracing a spectrum from how to hammer a nail, to how to make myself happy. A spectrum coherent, flowing, and unified. I learned how to build a house in which my physical self could live and I learned how to build a consciousness in which my spiritual self could exist. This quarter was the first in my thirteen years of school where community and environment were not contradicted but constructed."

Each day and week flowed along, providing new learning and experiences. It wasn't just designing and building, but cooking, foraging for mushrooms, herbs, mussels, and learning how to throw a beach seine for herring. It was sitting around the stove in the Ark telling stories, eating, playing guitars, singing and drumming, and learning to sharpen chisels for the next day's work. It was volleyball and yoga, trips to the beach, and talks by local artisans. It was working out group differences in communication, work habits, and cooperation.

FAR LEFT
Alan's cabin

ABOVE
Building the Ark.

LEFT
Group meeting.

As promised, we returned to campus to report to the rest of the school about our adventure. We brought with us a forty-page publication we had produced for sale, *Outlaw Building News*. Our collective presentation was a standing-room-only event with most of the audience wildly enthusiastic and some very hostile. For me and for most of the students in the class, it was a life-changing experience. It gave me the confidence and the vision to move forward with future courses in which everyone was both teacher and student.

energy pavilion

After several years' absence from Berkeley, I was encouraged to return to teaching on campus. The field course Making a Place in the Country had stimulated an approach to what I called Whole Systems Design. This approach calls for not just designing buildings but designing the essential life support components that go with them: energy, food production and nutrient recycling, water supply and reuse, and human waste disposal and recycling.

The U.S. space program was involved in a similar endeavor. In designing manned space vehicles in which humans would spend extended time in self-contained capsules beyond Earth's atmosphere, they were using the same language: life-support systems. The scientists and designers were figuring out how to design and integrate systems providing breathable air, energy, food, water, and human waste disposal for astronauts in weightless space with no atmosphere.

Other scholars and architects began researching and writing on the subject. Brenda Vale, an architect at Cambridge University in Great Britain, published a study, *The Autonomous House: Design and Planning for Self-Sufficiency,* and Tom Bender, professor of architecture at the University of Minnesota, was formulating plans for Project Oroborous, a demonstration house designed around concepts of energy and resource production, conservation, and recycling.

For the 1972–73 academic year, Jim Campe and I designed a yearlong course divided into three ten-week quarters. The focus of the class was to research, design, and build a self-sustaining model habitat. In the fall quarter, class members each researched the existing state-of-the-art, relevant life-support system designs, such as windmills to produce electricity, systems that could heat water using the sun, ways to recycle human wastes into nutrient-rich compost to grow food, methane generators that produced cooking gas from waste products, greenhouses to grow food year-round, and water-conserving devices. The collected information would be shared by the class.

In the winter quarter, each student prepared a design for a model habitat that integrated shelter with other life-support systems. At the end of the ten weeks, we would choose one design to build in the spring quarter. I posted the course description. Many students had heard about and read *Outlaw Building News,* our account of the Making a Place in the Country course. There was an enthusiastic response to the proposed year-long course, including several Vietnam veterans whose experiences lent a hard realism to our theoretical efforts.

The research quarter led us to nonacademic sources for information since searching the extensive university library system yielded few books or journals that covered the kinds of things we were looking for. For example, we could only find two books that even mentioned solar energy: Olgyay and Olgyay's *Solar Controls and Shading Devices,* and Farrington Daniel's *The Direct Use of the Sun's Energy.* New alternative magazines such as *Mother Earth News* and *The Whole Earth Catalog and Review* were sources and led us to a variety of backyard experiments.

The class put all our information into a 150-page document we called *The Natural Energy Handbook.* Since Earth Day 1970 and the emergence of a new back-to-the-land movement, interest in how to live lightly on the land without relying on large centralized systems and technologies was rapidly growing. Word got around and people wanted copies of the handbook, so we started printing and selling it. The local bookstores asked us for copies and we printed more. We banked the money we earned from selling our class notes to pay for our spring construction project.

In the shop we fabricated some systems, including primitive solar collectors for hot water. Students each developed their designs for an integrated habitat and we picked Jeff Poetsch's to build. Our plan was to build it outside near Wurster Hall, the home of UC Berkeley's College of Environmental Design.

The Energy Pavilion, built on the UC Berkeley campus in the spring of 1973, demonstrated the possibilities of energy-independent habitation.

Remembering People's Park, I walked our proposal through the appropriate channels. My department chair and dean were receptive and sent me to the chancellor's office. There I met with an assistant to the vice chancellor, who said it should be no problem. A scavenger friend told us about a large old barn in Hayward that we could tear down for the wood, and we piled into our mail van and Big Red, the flatbed truck, and spent several days dismantling the structure and de-nailing the wood. The dean assured us it was okay to build and we began construction on spring equinox in 1973.

The structure took shape quickly. The flat roof held our homemade solar collector, a pipe that transported rainwater to several fifty-five-gallon drums, and a small wind generator we had purchased. On the south side we built a small greenhouse of PVC pipe and a plastic cover and planted snow peas and lettuce in beds of compost we had made from donated food scraps from some local restaurants. Inside there was a composting privy, a urine collection system, and a sink with a water-conserving faucet that was supplied by the rainwater storage tanks. Outside, we had borrowed a stationary bicycle whose chain drove a food mill that ground grains or powered a small electric generator. Inside was covered with diagrams explaining the workings of all the systems.

We called our finished work the Energy Pavilion, since our focus had been on natural energy flows. The structure was completed in spring 1973 just as the OPEC oil embargo was creating angry long lines at gas stations, and people who previously took U.S. energy supplies and uses for granted were waking up to our dependence on centralized sources for all our basic needs.

Local television stations did stories about our Energy Pavilion demonstration project. Long lines of people queued up to tour the project. It was May and the semester was ending. In several weeks, parents and friends would be crowding onto the campus for graduation. In my school mailbox was a letter from the vice chancellor. It informed me that I had failed to submit my plan to the Campus Esthetics Committee, and, therefore, I would have to remove the structure within two weeks or the university administration would put a fence around it and take it down, and charge me for the cost of removal.

My hands shaking, my body cold with anger, I walked out into the warm sunlight and sat on a bench across from the Energy Pavilion where my students were conducting tours and trying to manage the patient crowd lined up to visit our contraption. A young man whom I did not recognize sat on the bench next to me. "I'm Harlow," he said. "You don't remember me, but I took your Ecological Design lecture course several years ago. Say, this pavilion is cool, but you don't look so happy. What's the matter?"

Still silent, I pulled the official letter from my pocket and handed it to him. "Shit," he said, "You don't have to put up with this. I'll give you money to do this kind of work outside the University. We'll go meet with my lawyer right now."

I went to my department office and filled out paperwork to take a leave of absence that was to last five years. And so I moved on to the next chapter of living and learning.

"Teach what you most want to learn." —Dick Price

In the 1960s, Esalen Institute cofounders Dick Price and Michael Murphy started an American cultural and intellectual revolution at Esalen Institute on the California coast near Big Sur. What they started became known as the human potential movement, an exploration of new ideas and practices in psychology, philosophy, and the marriage of body and mind. Dick's maxim was certainly the rule, particularly in the early years. Their teachers and workshop students broke all the rules of the academy, letting the chips fall where they might—not always a pretty sight. But Dick's admonition to explore what you most want to and need to know through sharing your learning with others has always been my path.

integral urban house

The year spent developing the Energy Pavilion and *The Natural Energy Handbook* had put me in touch with many people who were interested in participating in our type of design. Among them were Bill and Helga Olkowski, who were experimenting with their own home and yard in Berkeley. Bill was an entomologist who was working on integrated pest management at the university. The news that Farallones Institute had received funding to continue our experiments and demonstrations in ecologically appropriate design got around to the Olkowskis and they contacted me. Sterling Bunnell, a psychiatrist and naturalist who taught at the California College of Arts and Crafts, came to visit. A roundish, disheveled-looking man, Sterling soon enthralled me with his knowledge of natural history and processes. No detail was too small to escape his notice, no time span too large to discourse on. He would describe Berkeley's geological history in minute detail, and then shift to the structure of a raptor's eye, his own experiment with pooping in a pot filled with red worms, or sending his children out to collect road kills that he would prepare for dinner. And then there was Art Boericke, an itinerant carpenter and writer who was going around the West with Barry Shapiro, documenting the handmade houses being built by back-to-the-landers along the California coast and its backwoods.

Sim's first sketch connecting natural energy flows to human needs through ecologically appropriate technology.

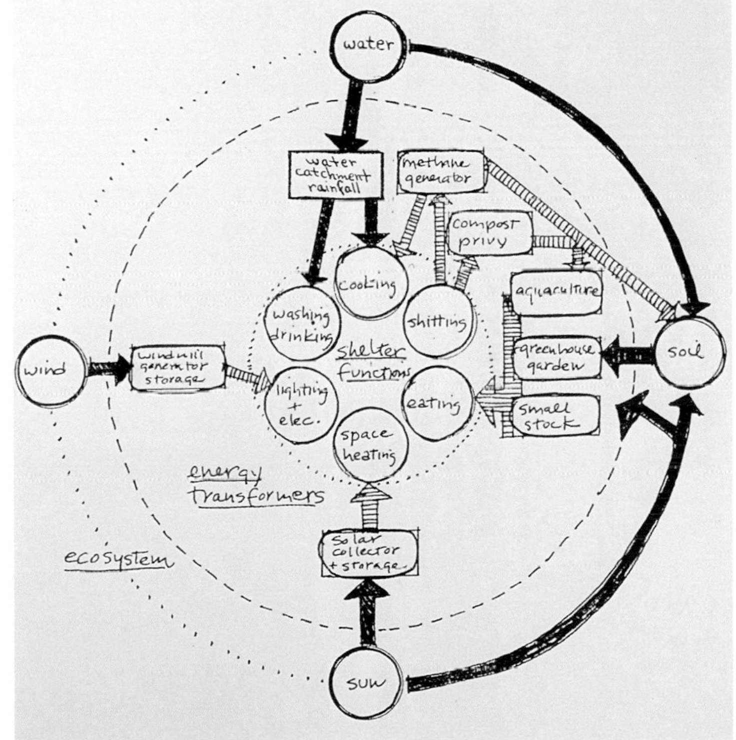

At a lively meeting of the core group and our funder, Harlow Daugherty, we discussed where and what our first project should be. Many people at that time seemed to be giving up on city living, attempting to reconnect to the earth by moving to rural areas. Bill and Helga argued persuasively for an urban demonstration project. "Cities are where the people are. Everyone can't move to the country. If people move to the country with their urban ways and expectations, the country will be transformed into the city. The challenge is to make cities ecologically stable and healthy places to live."

After more discussion, I was asked to locate an existing house for our first demonstration project. The Olkowskis' main demand was that the lot have good soil. So we focused on a run-down Berkeley neighborhood where the alluvial soils from the hills had been deposited on the flats next to San Francisco Bay. I found an old Victorian whose last use was a drug rehab center. We purchased the house and big lot for $8,000. I hired Jim Campe, Scott Matthews, and Jeff Poetsch, who had all worked on the Energy Pavilion, and Tom Javits, the Olkowskis' assistant, to work with me to plan and then start building.

I drew a diagram, which became the basis for our thinking about the interconnections among functional needs, on-site natural resources, and possible appropriate technologies that could channel energy, nutrient, and waste flows.

In the first months of designing and building, there were almost daily conflicts bred by the perspective of our own particular specialties. Tom and Jim almost came to blows over how the concrete floor would be poured. Jim, with his builder's background, wanted to bring the concrete truck down the driveway for the pour. Tom vowed to lay his body in front of the wheels before he would allow the precious soil to be compacted, and have the life squeezed out of it. So we wheel-barrowed in many yards of concrete by hand until our blisters were too painful to continue. Everyone began to learn that creating an Integral House means sharing an integral language and image that transcend the narrow jargon of discrete disciplines. The builders learned that a gram of what they called "dirt" was home to millions of living bacteria that processed organic matter into usable nutrients for plants. Tom learned that concrete is heavy and dries fast. Should we cut a tree to allow more sun to fall on our solar hot water collectors? Was space to store wood scraps more important than space for the chickens?

Starting to rebuild the old house. Solar greenhouse is on the left.

LEFT
The Integral Urban House.

BELOW
The Integral Urban House site plan.

LOWER LEFT
Rabbit pens with vermiculture below.

LOWER RIGHT
The first urban composting toilet.

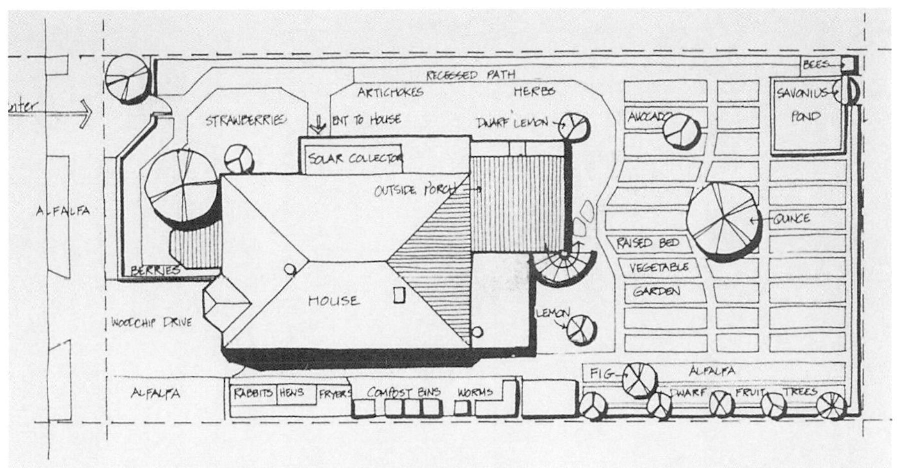

As we argued and learned from each other, the house and site started to take shape. On the south, we added a greenhouse to the lower floor entrance and exhibit space. The sidewalk was torn up and mulch spread to make more habitat for microorganisms. We planted a French intensive raised-bed garden—then still a novelty. In its center, we planted the bowl of the house's flush toilet, replaced by California's first urban composting toilet. We built small pens for chickens and rabbits along the north side of the house. The rabbit pens were located over the chicken run so that the rabbit manure fell into the chicken yard where it would be picked over. Both rabbits and chickens subsisted largely on weeds pulled from the garden. Next to the rabbits and chickens we located the triple compost bins and fly traps whose contents were fed to the chickens. In the corner of the lot were beehives and a small aquaculture pond. This arrangement allowed dead bees to fall into the pond where they were consumed by the fish. A windmill built out of recycled oil drums operated a mechanical pump that lifted water into a biological filter.

Inside the house we installed a number of energy-conserving and passive solar features. Against an interior window, we installed racks of recycled gallon glass jugs to collect solar heat. The kitchen stove was combination gas and wood, burning scraps and prunings. It took about a year to complete the house and get all systems running.

UC Berkeley students served as interns and residents with the task of operating all systems and keeping careful records, including measuring what the home and its occupants produced and consumed. Getting accurate quantitative data on the inputs and outputs of the energy, resource recycling, and food production systems was an important responsibility of the residents. Residents

The completed Integral Urban House.

also tracked six cycles: the human food-compost cycle, human waste cycle, urine cycle, small stock cycle, urine aquatic cycle, and insect food cycle. We operated the house for a ten-year period with resident interns cycling through and a constant stream of workshops and visitor tours.

Much of what we learned was published in 1979 by Sierra Club Books as *The Integral Urban House: Self-Reliant Living in the City.* It is unfortunate that the book is now out of print, because the feedback I've received over the years is that this book is perhaps the best and most complete guide to the theory of creating integral ecologic systems at the household scale. The book contains the earliest and most complete explanation and diagrams of how to approach the design of ecological systems with the four main features:

- Process materials and energy through closed loops and multiple channels.
- Release energy in the system in small increments.
- Maintain a steady state through negative feedback loops and permeable boundaries.
- Store information in diffuse elements.

Many of the experimental systems did not work well or generated certain issues within the community. The bees had a hard time surviving the pollution from the nearby freeway and industrial plants. Indeed, our experiment and monitoring woke up Berkeley residents and officials to the extent and diversity of pollution in West Berkeley. The aquatic system was too small and never successful. Growing and eating our own protein through a rabbit and chicken food chain infuriated many vegetarians. Until our Board no longer permitted it, Tom Javits would end public talks by stroking a cute bunny, breaking its neck, and skinning it on the spot. Tens of thousands of people visited the house during its ten years of operation and were inspired by what they experienced. The Olkowskis were right: You need to change people where they live—in cities.

LEFT
Cover of *The Integral Urban House: Self-Reliant Living In the City.*

BELOW
Integral Urban House tour.

"Farallones Institute's *Integral Urban House: Self Reliant Living in the City* is a magnificent, inspiring record of eco-technically effective intelligent human cooperation. . . . This is magnificent news for humanity. We are on our way."

—R. Buckminster Fuller

the farallones rural center

"We design self-sustaining living patterns that increase our awareness of and balance between the realities of Nature and the needs of Man."

—Farallones Institute Brochure, 1974

Farallones solar cabins.

While the Integral Urban House was under construction, some of us were already hatching a larger project. Harlow Daugherty, our principal funder, was interested in having us try our hand at designing and constructing a place that could be an example of integrating the systems that we were building at the Integral Urban House on the scale of a rural village, a community that would be home to staff and students. Already living in the country, I didn't need much convincing. We began a long search for the right place.

David Donnelley was the cofounder of the School of Arts and Sciences, a fine private high school my daughter was attending. He had an eighty-acre ranch near Occidental, a small town in western Sonoma County not far from the coast. It offered a diverse hilly landscape of redwoods, apple orchards, and grazing land. I presented the prospectus for a Farallones Rural Center to him and he liked it. "My family isn't really using the place. We'll let your organization use it with an option to purchase when you're ready."

The site consisted of rolling hills bisected by a stream and bordered by several acres of flat fields and beautiful oaks. The only buildings were a low-ceilinged cabin and a sagging garage. The back meadows showed traces of furrows where wine grapes had been planted many years before. Several ancient fruit trees still bore determinedly. Here we wanted to establish a community, an experiment, and a school for ecological design. After several trips to get the lay of the land, my next stop was the Sonoma County Planning Department. The county had been doing battle for some years with a commune in the area: Morning Star Ranch, owned by folksinger Lou Gottlieb. The county claimed the place had many illegal buildings and inadequate waste and water facilities. It also was an alleged haven for other forms of countercultural experimentation.

I assured them we were not another Morning Star, but rather a nonprofit educational institute whose mission was to design, teach, and build a center that demonstrated more environmentally friendly designs for rural living, integrating shelter, food, energy, water, and waste systems. "Make an application for a use permit, and submit a master plan," they replied.

I prepared and submitted a plan that showed a kitchen/dining building, a bathhouse, and composting toilets. Staff and students would live in tents until we could build permanent facilities. Months went by; no word from the county. I would call and they'd say, "We're looking at it."

Finally, we had a meeting with the planning director. "We can classify you as an organized camp," he said and handed me the regulations for an organized camp. One sentence stuck out. "Water Supply: 120 gallons/person/day." With twenty students and ten staff that meant four thousand gallons per day.

I pointed to the regulation. "Our whole purpose is to design to use less. We're designing for no more than fifteen gallons per person per day, including our food systems. We're not having flush toilets, and all the shower and kitchen water will be recycled into the garden."

LEFT
Farallones garden.

RIGHT
Sim Van der Ryn turning the compost privy pile.

The director replied, "No exceptions to the rule. And moreover, we don't allow outhouses, or whatever you call them, or gray water. You need to revise your applications to meet our rules before we can even review them."

It was March 1975. We were designing and advertising our first programs to begin in June. Our first advertised program at the Rural Center offered a two-month residential program or one-year apprenticeship called Whole Life Systems in the areas of our expertise: building design and construction, farming and gardening, energy systems, ecosystem management, and community living skills. At the time, our hands-on experiential, learn-by-doing methodology was unusual to college-level education. Making a Place in the Country had lit the vision and convinced me it could work.

A quote from our first program brochure highlights the intent of our program: "During the course of the year, we will be sharing our experience and skills towards developing a simpler, more integrated way of life. . . . Our emphasis is on bringing together theory and practice. Learning how seemingly different disciplines are closely related. Helping people develop a world view which will contribute to their personal growth and professional competence."

The mailings to colleges were going out soon. I'd hired Jim Campe and several former Zen Center carpenters, whose work I greatly admired, to start building the first structures with materials we reclaimed from San Francisco piers being demolished. David Katz, a young farmer and UC Davis agriculture graduate, came to start the garden and farm operation. I didn't call the county again. We started building, recruited other staff, prepared our mailings, and waited for potential students to return their applications.

We didn't have to wait long. Our only advertising other than word of mouth was a poster mailed to two hundred schools of architecture and design. Soon we had scores of applications for our first summer program. We selected twenty students with diverse backgrounds. Like the staff, most of them were in their twenties.

Beyond the vision of a rural, whole-systems village, there was no master site plan. The kitchen/dining building, compost privy, and solar showers were completed. The group gathered the first day and decided our priorities were the garden, which David had already begun, converting the old garage into a shop and expanding it to include a visitors' center and library and a solar bathhouse.

ABOVE
Farallones Institute barn raising.

FACING PAGE
Farallones solar cabins.

The south slope next to the shop became "solar suburbia" when I hired a young Santa Cruz designer/builder, Peter Calthorpe, who initiated a project to build five passive solar cabins to be used for staff housing. Each cabin was designed with a different passive solar technique and was monitored for energy production and consumption using equipment provided by our utility, Pacific Gas and Electric. The experiment was the first comparative testing of different residential solar heating and cooling techniques in the United States.

Michael Stusser joined the staff as head gardener. He had worked and trained with English-born Alan Chadwick, who was recognized as the father of the French intensive gardening method. Instead of row crop cultivation, this method uses raised beds rich with compost, and solid planting of edible vegetables for high yields, and low maintenance. It uses no herbicides, pesticides, or nonorganic fertilizers. Michael was a master "chef du compost." The clay soils gradually became rich and fragrant with humus. We began growing a selection of heirloom varieties of vegetables unknown to commercial farmers alongside beautiful flowering plants.

Sonoma County officials, aware that we had begun our project without obtaining the required planning or building permits, moved forward with legal action against the Farallones Institute and me as its president, planner, and architect. We were cited for some 224 violations of county and state regulations. The health department found the composting toilets and "milk from an unauthorized source" (the Institute's Jersey cow) particularly egregious. In the fall of 1975 I left for Sacramento, the legal issues unresolved. But as word spread that we were not a hippie commune, we gained local political support and media coverage. The county backed off through face-saving measures on both sides.

Some of the best students stayed on as apprentices, and some filled staff positions. Several dry years made water development and conservation priorities so we added a new well and twenty thousand gallons of storage. Using funding from a soil conservation district grant, we constructed a large pond for erosion control and irrigation. A large barn built of reclaimed lumber was built by one summer's building class. A daylong barn raising with several hundred people participating was a thrilling experience—community building in the fullest sense.

New Alchemy Institute on Cape Cod, founded by John and Nancy Todd, and the Farallones Institute became the two best-known centers in the country for learning about and applying ecologically appropriate technologies.

My own day-to-day involvement on-site ended when I joined Governor Brown's administration in 1975. I continued on the Farallones board as founder and president. The biggest continuing problem was grappling with the contradictions inherent in a context where residents were both members of a living community and also employees of an institution they didn't control. As Allison Dykstra, a former center director, put it, "The long-term effectiveness and sustainability of systems is also dependent on social contexts and forms."

In addition to our summer residential program and apprenticeships, we added many more programs serving a wide variety of audiences. Weekend and weeklong gardening workshops teaching new organic methods and workshops in Community Technology were added. In 1979, the U.S. Peace Corps asked us to develop their first program in "Appropriate Technology and Renewable Energy." Peace Corps volunteers were sent to the Rural Center for intensive preservice training before their assignment overseas. Farallones staff traveled abroad to conduct follow-up training for volunteers and their local counterparts.

Farallones attracted staff with great expertise in issues facing the developing nations. In 1983, Farallones International was formed to provide consulting and training services in Africa, South America, and the Caribbean. "Power in Your Hands" was developed to introduce primary and secondary students and their teachers to practical applications of ecology to life and to school curriculum.

The Peace Corps had become the major income source. During an inspection trip to the center, a Reagan administration representative noticed a poster of Che Guevara on a staff office wall. Shortly thereafter, the Peace Corps abruptly terminated our contract. In the 1980s our philosophy and practices were not attracting new adherents. A majority of the board was reluctant to face the new reality and cut staff and expenses. We were deeply in debt.

TOP
Peter Calthorpe monitors solar performance of cabins.

MIDDLE
Kids working in the Farallones Garden drying apples.

BOTTOM
Gardener Michelle

ABOVE
Garden and greenhouse.

A new board, with me reinstalled as president, considered turning the Farallones Institute Rural Center into a more conventional retreat center, a venue for people who had established programs and markets. After ten years, what was thriving, beautiful, and the biggest attraction to the Rural Center was the garden, which, under the artistic and knowledgeable hands of Doug Gosling, had become one of the most acclaimed food and flower gardens in northern California.

In the late eighties, the new form emerged. A group of friends in Occidental, including an accomplished painter, a community organizer, several teachers, and Doug Gosling, purchased the site to live and work on. In turn they leased the land to their own new nonprofit Occidental Arts and Ecology Center. In this way, the ever-present contradiction between responsibility to the institute's mission and community residency was resolved. Today, the center carries on the Farallones tradition with hands-on education, primarily in gardening and permaculture, some alternative building workshops, and painting and other arts. Now the landscape of the center, so lovingly nurtured for over twenty-five years, is healthier and more beautiful than ever.

"Living with Appropriate Technology"
By Paul Hawken

Excerpt from *The Farallones Institute: Creating Tools for a Convivial Society,* Annual Report, 1979.

From the outset Rural Center has been concerned with creating a community of architects, scientists, biologists, carpenters, craftspersons, and gardeners who could evolve a living system within what is being called appropriate technology. Designing a composting toilet that works is one problem; living with it, and other people, is another. Most of the people who moved onto the land at the Rural Center assumed that they were building a center of experimentation, learning, and demonstration. While these activities can be—and are being—carried on, the group is also learning that a group of people is a society, and that, in the words of *RAIN* magazine's Tom Bender, the best technology is ultimately a good society; yet this is the hardest technology of all to create.

The Rural Center devotes most of its teaching activities to hands-on pursuits, instructing apprentices how to apply appropriate technology in everyday life. To date the main focuses have been intensive agriculture, the raising of small livestock, solar house design and construction (using recycled and indigenous materials), and the development of household water systems stressing grey water use and composting toilets.

Farallones is carefully examining all aspects of daily life—in a sense, taking them apart and putting them back together again. The water we drink: How much do we use, how best to heat it, where does it come from, and where does it go? Our food: How much do we need, what kind, from where, how best to grow, process, cook, and eat it? Our waste: How much do we waste (water, electricity, solids), and how could it be used more efficiently and safely? Our houses: What designs and materials are best, what size, how to heat them and minimize inefficiency and waste? Our landscape: How to make it work both for us and for the local ecology, which kinds of landscapes are productive and which consumptive? Our animals: How to feed them, keep them, and share spaces with them? And, finally, how can we do all this in a cyclical, interrelated, synergetic way, elegant in its simplicity and practical enough so that more than the rich can afford to conserve? Those are the relevant questions, and Farallones is attempting to answer these questions by living through them.

I remember having dinner with David Sillman, the carpenter at the Rural Center who designed and built a sixteen-by-twenty-one-foot house with post-and-lintel construction, stucco walls (both interior and exterior), with an attached greenhouse, and a drum-wall passive heating storage system—all for under $1,500 in materials cost. He used recycled wood and windows, along with handmade tiles fired at the Rural Center. In a cautious and probing manner, David inquired what I meant by terms such as right livelihood and voluntary simplicity. It was like a Hopi asking, "What is culture?" There wasn't an answer I could give that would come close to the questioner's experience.

chapter 4

SECOND GENERATION ECOLOGICAL DESIGN

"Will we muster the intelligence and love, to craft a future that all living beings can share? This is the choice each of us makes everyday."

—L. Hunter Lovins, 2004

sacramento

While I was still at Farallones in Occidental, I received a call from Jerry Brown, newly elected governor of California. He asked me what I thought about rebuilding the state capitol building, which seismic safety experts said could fall down in a quake. I said I didn't know enough about it. I asked him if he'd read the British economist E.F. Schumacher's book, *Small is Beautiful,* which had recently been published. The book argues that the western economy is stuck on large-scale growth, which isn't good for cultures, people, economies, or ecology. What we need, argues Schumacher, are humane, ecologically, and locally appropriate technologies. The governor said he would read the book and call back in a few weeks.

A few weeks later Governor Brown called and asked me to come to Sacramento to discuss the state capitol rebuilding project and write a report for him, which I did. I felt the project was a political boondoggle, and that the structural studies didn't confirm the seismic risk. I also noted that the state had a large shortfall of state-owned office space, and money could be better spent on constructing new state office space. This was far cheaper than leasing space from the private sector, which the Reagan administration had done. Then on my own, I wrote two other papers that I sent to him. The first, "Notes on State Energy Policy," argued that the newly formed State Energy Commission should focus on conservation and renewable energy. The second paper, "Appropriate Technology and State Government," argued that the Governor's Office could encourage low-cost experiments and demonstration projects that followed Schumacher's ideas and others in the growing ecologically appropriate technology movement.

The energy shock of 1973 was still very much on people's minds; much like 9/11 has been in recent years. I suggested that "mass institutions and economies based on cheap energy and resources are going to be transformed, regardless of our value system . . .," and warned that if they don't, "one can picture another scenario: as things become tighter and fear grips the dependent urban mass, large corporations and government assume total control, doling out thinner slices of a dwindling pie, and spending ever more to maintain control and order in an inherently unstable situation."

The paper proposed establishing an Office of Appropriate Technology (OAT) within the Governor's Office. "The purpose of this office will be to nurture and encourage technology appropriate to sustain a society of finite resources at a human scale." The paper goes on to give twenty-nine specific examples in which appropriate technology could be applied through state initiatives in the areas of natural environment, waste and resource management, food production, transportation, housing and energy consumption, and industry.

I visualized the office as having the multiple functions of providing information to consumers, making visible specific working examples, extending appropriate technology by working with state agencies to remove administrative and legal barriers. "In most areas of life—housing, education, professional training, health, water, waste management, transportation, banking . . . OAT will seek out and document overt and covert subsidies of wasteful practices and deterrents to local self-reliance." In other words, I saw OAT as a David in the Governor's Office that would take on the Goliath of special interests that benefited from subsidies and regulations such as encouraging agribusiness through water subsidies, wasteful building codes, and health codes preventing water conservation and biological waste treatment.

Meanwhile, Farallones Institute was in the midst of its first summer program. Things were going well, with construction of solar staff cabins and a rapidly expanding garden moving along. The permitting issues with the county were escalating. All summer I was very conflicted between my commitment to making Farallones a major alternative center for change, or jumping into trying to change the way public design and construction was done if I was offered a job in the Brown Administration. Soon I heard from the Governor offering to appoint me California State Architect.

I told Governor Brown that I was interested in being an advisor to him on the issues discussed in my energy and appropriate technology papers. He said that I would be in a more powerful role running a line agency with a large staff and large construction budget, and he would support a major program of building new energy-efficient office buildings. Again, I expressed my fear of becoming a bureaucrat, exactly the kind of folks who were trying to crush Farallones. He responded with an ironic laugh. "Ah, the embarrassment of power! Don't you get it? Sacramento is just a sandbox for us to play in. You can go for what you want. You'll have to sell your plan to the legislature. I'm with you. Just don't get me in trouble, or you're out."

So at the end of the summer I moved to Sacramento, a block from the ugly two-story building that housed the main office of the Office of Architecture and Construction, which I soon renamed the Office of the State Architect so people could identify with a person, rather than a faceless bureaucracy.

Sim Van der Ryn in the Office of the State Architect, Sacramento, California, 1975. Photograph © Art Rogers.

Over drinks in our apartment across the street from my office my first week on the job, Resources secretary Clare Deitrich, a former Sierra Club official, gave me the most valuable one-sentence advice I received in Sacramento: "Whatever you're going to do, get it going the first six months or else you won't get going at all."

There were four main items on my agenda. The first was to push through a program to build seven new state office buildings in Sacramento and other major cities that would be models of energy efficiency and provide a more humane face to employees and the public. The second was to rebuild a new mixed-use community on state-owned land around the state capitol, much of which had been torn down in an ill-fated state redevelopment effort when Pat Brown was governor. The third item was to develop a building code designed just for remote rural areas that would encourage living more lightly on the land, not requiring all the suburban accessories that put a huge money burden on people who wanted to live simply, and not put a huge ecological burden on rural land and its resource base. And finally, to establish a focus on appropriate technology at the state government level.

Sacramento is a grid city, with numbered streets running north and south and lettered streets running east and west. A square block between 8th and 9th streets and P and Q streets had been cleared. This was to be the site for our first new state office building. I decided it should be a low-rise building configured to fit the street pattern. While my office had a large design and production staff, I brought in a team of young designers to work with me—the first vanguard of solar and climate responsive designers. Peter Calthorpe came from Farallones. Former graduate students Scott Matthews and Bruce Corson came from Berkeley. We developed a plan for a square building with a large interior courtyard lit by north-facing sawtooth monitors; the way old industrial buildings were day-lit. We did a careful climate analysis that showed that on summer days, when Sacramento was fiercely hot (often over 100 degrees), in the evenings the ocean influence drifting up the Sacramento River cooled the evenings down. Many of the old houses were built with exhaust fans in the attic. With this plan, all offices would be close to natural daylight, either from the windows facing the street or from the atrium. For the east and west façades, we developed external shades operated by a microprocessor that lowered the shades automatically to keep out the direct rays of the sun between May and October. The building would be the first major building in the United States designed to adapt to climate and save energy.

The plan took shape quickly—at least by government standards—and six months after arriving in Sacramento I was ready to seek the legislature's approval to build the first building and budget for six more in Sacramento, San Francisco, Long Beach, and San Jose. I went to the legislative committee in charge of capital expenditures, bringing with me a gallon gas can, a Japanese teacup, and first sketches of the building.

Starting my presentation, I held up the gas can. "The energy equivalent of this gallon can is how much energy it takes to cool, heat, and light a square foot of today's state office buildings, or 140,000 BTU."

Picking up the teacup I said, "In our new buildings, our analysis shows we will reduce the energy consumption from that gallon can to this teacup: an 80 percent reduction." In 1975, the oil embargo and shortages of 1973 was still very much on everyone's mind. My presentation made an impression even on the most conservative legislators.

The budget analyst who was assigned to oversee my office argued that the four-story, open atrium space was wasted space. I replied it was the lungs of the building. Instead of relying solely on air-conditioning, we would have windows that opened, shades that automatically came down over the windows on the east and west sides, and large fans in the atrium that would flush out warm air at night when energy consumption was lowest. Heat was stored in the concrete mass of the building, so the temperature would rise slowly, and then the mass of the building would cool down again at night.

After some heated discussion, the chairwoman of the committee, a flinty conservative woman from a rural county, said, “I think we should give this young man a chance. Maybe his ideas will work.” We were in business. Now we had to test our ideas. Computer models that simulated the thermal performance of buildings were just starting to be developed. We were dealing with an area of fluid dynamics—heat transfer and climate adaptation—that mechanical engineers didn’t know much about. Bruce Corson and his friend Bruce Wilcox, another former graduate student, began work on a computer model that could simulate the building’s thermal performance. We labored to work out the myriad details of the building, involving a team of state architects who were starved for some change in their usual routine.

The computer model showed that the building interior temperature would hover around seventy-eight degrees on the hottest summer days and sixty-five degrees in the winter. The State Employees Union leader protested, pointing out that their work contract called for buildings that remained a steady sixty-eight degrees year round. We wound up monitoring a series of state buildings in Sacramento for a year and found out that on an average, they were sixty-five degrees in the summer and seventy-eight degrees in winter! We won that argument.

Maintenance people were opposed to operable windows, a key feature of the design. Instead of intense overall artificial lighting, we went to modest background lighting, suggesting that if people needed more light, they use desk lamps. At the time, it was not unusual for one switch to control the lighting on an entire large floor. Lights were kept on twenty-four hours a day. Resource secretary Huey Johnson, the founder of Trust for Public Land, sent me a note asking if his sealed high-rise building could also have windows that opened. I sent him a gift-wrapped river boulder the size of a softball with a note, “Use this to open your window.”

Jerry and I had decided to name the building in honor of Gregory Bateson, a mentor to both of us who had died shortly before the building was completed. Here is what I said at the dedication in 1980:

“Most of Gregory’s life was spent trying to illuminate the wholeness that is in man and the natural world. We are all part of what Gregory called ‘the pattern that connects.’ In the last month of his life, I asked him what single thing was needed for people to grasp a new way of looking at their world. ‘People are mad for quantity, yet what is significant is difference,’ he said. And so it is with this building named in his honor.”

FACING
Gregory Bateson Building,
Sacramento, California.
Photograph © Cathy Kelly, 1984, 1999.

LEFT
Gregory Bateson Building, atrium,
Photograph © Donald Corner.

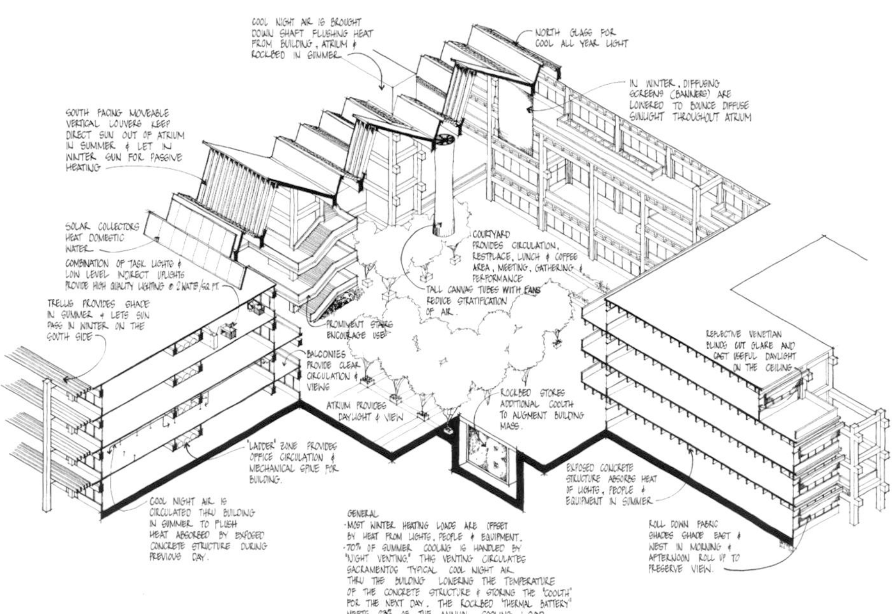

Bateson Building diagram

We found that in designing with natural energy flows we became sensitive to difference. The measure became not foot-candles of quantifiable illumination, which means nothing, but the quality of light you experience, which means everything. We found we could consider the wall of the building not as a static, two-dimensional architectural element, but as a living skin that is sensitive to and adapts to differences in temperature and light. We found that designing a building to save energy means designing a building that is sensitive to difference and results in a building that is better for people. We are not adapted to live or work at temperatures or lighting levels that are uniform or constant. We are most alive when we experience subtle cycles of difference in our surroundings. The building itself becomes "the pattern which connects" us to the change and flow of climate, season, sun, shadow, constantly tuning our awareness of the natural cycles that support all life.

Maybe this is what esthetics and beauty are all about. Maybe what we find beautiful is that which connects us to an experience of difference: to an experience of the patterns of wholeness, patterns that distinguish the living world from the works of humankind.

Based on the experience of designing the first energy-efficient state building, I decided to have a statewide competition to award the next buildings we would build. With funding from the State Energy Commission, we prepared a program requiring that each design submittal provide a detailed energy analysis using our newly developed tools. The competition, with the prize of a commission to design major new buildings, introduced California's architects to the new tools of energy-efficient design based on responsiveness to site and climate. Within ten years, these concepts and new regulations for commercial and residential buildings made California the most energy-efficient state in the nation for buildings built during and after the Brown administration.

the capitol area plan

Within downtown Sacramento, the state owned an area of 120 acres, approximately half of it occupied by existing state buildings. The remainder was largely surface parking for state employees and a few remaining houses and apartments that survived Governor Brown Sr.'s 1960 redevelopment plan, which envisioned nothing but high-rise government buildings. Our goal was to create a mixture of new low-rise state buildings and new low-rise housing and services, laced together with open space and trees to cool the intense valley summers. We wanted to reintroduce diversity into what had become a government enclave.

Biology teaches us that complexity and diversity increase the chances for a living system's survival. Cities and their inhabitants are no exception to the rule, although we were fighting fifty years of rigid, modernist grand plans (such as Le Corbusier's plan to destroy the texture of Paris with monolithic, high-rise towers). Our Capitol Area Plan was designed to develop incrementally with enough flexibility to adapt to changing needs. It was a set of guidelines rather than a rigid image of what the future form should be.

A joint powers authority was formed between the state and the city of Sacramento to develop vacant state land. The amount of land in surface parking created an urban heat island as the asphalt soaked up the summer heat. We worked out an arrangement where employees would park under the freeway that ringed the core of Sacramento. The New Capitol Area Authority, staffed in part by UC graduate students I had brought up to learn and work, developed a plan that started by repairing many state-owned apartment buildings and houses. Other sites were designated for new developer-built housing. (After leaving government service, my new office, Van der Ryn Calthorpe and Associates, designed the first of these new projects, Somerset Park.) Now thirty years later, the monoculture has been transformed into a diverse polyculture. A light rail runs through the district, old buildings have been rehabilitated, and new human-scale spaces and buildings abound. It may not be Paris, but it is a better, more livable Sacramento neighborhood.

office of appropriate technology (OAT)

The governor did establish the Office of Appropriate Technology, known by its acronym, OAT, in May of 1976 by an executive order to "assist and advise the governor and all state agencies in developing and implementing less costly and less energy intensive technologies of recycling, waste disposal, transportation, agriculture, energy, and building design."

The office started small, initially focusing on assembling information on appropriate technologies useful to consumers. We developed a mobile version of the Integral Urban House concept that traveled to state and county fairs. We began a program to train solar technicians to install solar hot water systems and retrofit state-owned apartments, starting with the building in which the governor lived.

A personal favorite of mine was the bicycle program. Reviewing the Office of the State Architect's budget, I noticed we were spending a great deal of money on taxis to ferry employees short distances to other state offices. I went to the Sacramento Police bicycle auction and bought fifty bikes for five dollars each, had them painted white, and applied a State of California seal on each. Then we had bike racks installed at every state building within a two-mile radius of the capitol building. A memo went out to all agencies that cab rides under two miles were not permitted except on extremely hot or cold days, and that all staff without disabilities should use the bikes. I'd gotten the idea from the free white bikes in Amsterdam, and from our nearby neighbors in Davis, where bikes were a primary means of transportation on their flat campus. We garnered a lot of publicity for the program and people started to take notice of OAT.

These are my three treasures,
guard them well.

The first is compassion,
the inner limit.

The second is frugality,
the outer limit.

The third is the desire not to be
foremost under heaven.

— Lao Tsu

Lao Tzu on an Office of Appropriate Technology poster.

At a policy level, OAT got involved in studying ways to implement direct marketing for small farmers, resulting in legislation enabling farmers' markets in every county. This resulted from the frustration of a growing number of small new organic farmers who could find no outlet for their products.

In Arcata, in Humboldt County, I supported the funding of a biological wastewater marsh treatment project, defeating a fifty-million-dollar sewer bond issue. This was an important breakthrough. Thirty years later, the marsh on Humboldt Bay is a beautiful, ecologically rich, natural area, treating sewage safely and at a fraction of the cost of the ugly, concrete, conventional secondary treatment plant.

OAT grew in size and influence. Two close friends—Wilson Clark, an iconoclastic and brilliant young energy expert who was the governor's energy advisor, and Bill Press, Director of the State Office of Planning—and I provided policy direction.

Director Bob Judd managed a diverse staff of thirty. My initial vision was fulfilled as OAT increasingly worked with local government and community groups, coordinating projects on a wide variety of projects promoting the use of resource- and energy-conserving technologies and practices, and community self-reliance. After Brown left office in 1982, the new Republican governor eliminated OAT.

The final item on my Sacramento agenda was to reform building codes for rural areas. The codes seemed unnecessarily restrictive, designed for mass-produced suburbs with infrastructure such as sewers, electrical grids, and unlimited water. My own experience building in Inverness and at Occidental, and the bureaucratic horror stories conveyed to me by the new rural migrants trying to build simple homes in the country using their own labor, convinced me we needed a special code designed for rural owner-builders, not suburban consumers.

A political constituency was forming, particularly in Mendocino County, where new residents formed a group they called United Stand. They started visiting me in Sacramento to devise a plan. By now, my secretary, Rita, was used to rural folk showing up in their quaint clothes and long hair, sometimes without shoes, which is where she would draw the line, writing me a memo insisting that visitors to my office were required by OSHA to wear shoes. I had the habit of taking off my shoes as soon as I got to work and wandering around the office in my stocking feet. My staff was amazingly tolerant and supportive. They'd never experienced anyone like me, and my style was drawing positive attention to their formerly faceless office. They seemed to enjoy the notoriety and media attention that the office and I received. Ever the teacher, I instituted a noon lecture series where various notables in our movement came by to speak. Folks from other state agencies, journalists, and local colleges started to join in.

Working with the State Department of Housing and Community Development, we drew up a simplified code for owner-built rural homes, called Class K. Most controversial was the provision that houses did not have to have a flush toilet. Alternate systems such as composting toilets were acceptable. Many of the rural sites where people were settling had limited water, which people wanted to reserve for growing food, not for flushing down a toilet and into a septic tank. Many people were building composting toilets from the design I had created and installed some years earlier at Farallones. County health departments viewed the State Architect and his composting toilet as a menace equal to the Black Plague.

Gift from OAT staff to Sim Van der Ryn.

Working with John Bryson, head of the State Water Quality Control Board and the State Health Director, we designed a program to grant experimental permits for composting toilets if they would participate in a three-year, state-funded study to evaluate their performance and potential health risks. On a meeting one Monday morning after spending the weekend at Farallones, I brought in a jar of well-aged compost from our composting toilet at the Institute. With a flourish, I dumped it on the potted plant in the Health Director's office. "There's the beginning of our study. Let me know how the plant likes the compost and call me if you get sick." Chuckles all around. I had made my point. The state passed Class K and with a great deal of politicking, the coastal rural counties adopted the regulations, and many technically illegal handmade houses became legal. People no longer had to fear the dreaded red tag posted by roving building inspectors, which could lead to the demolition of their handcrafted homes, many of which were works of true beauty.

After a very busy, eventful four years, with the items on my initial agenda well on their way to success, I felt ready to go. We'd been living in a little Sacramento bungalow a few blocks from the capitol. The governor, who lived in a small apartment nearby, was a frequent last-minute visitor, bringing guests or other staff for hastily prepared meals, after which we would enjoy Brown-style Socratic dialogues that flitted like a hummingbird alighting on diverse subjects, extracting their intellectual nectar, and then moving on to the next. Jerry loved to cook up "a yeasty intellectual ferment," as he used to say, and there were always interesting people and conversations going on late into the night. There were late summer night jaunts to riverfront dives perched over the broad banks of the Sacramento. Brown had made a quick stab at the 1976 Democratic presidential primaries, and as 1980 approached, he seemed more serious about running again. His playful and open style was becoming more guarded and calculating. It was time to go, to return to Inverness, to Farallones Institute, and to teaching.

marin solar village

After leaving Sacramento at the end of Jerry Brown's first term with the key goals of my agenda accomplished or underway, I returned to Inverness and to teaching after a four-year absence. Berkeley Chancellor Mike Heyman had called while I was in Sacramento, reminding me that four years was the longest leave the university could grant, so it was either time to return to teaching or resign. I chose to go back to teaching and continue as president of Farallones Institute, which was thriving.

Excerpt from *The CoEvolution Quarterly.* Published by the *Whole Earth Catalog,* Summer 1979.

By Stuart Brand

Candor was what made Sim Van der Ryn one of Jerry Brown's best appointments. At the time (1975) it was seen as one of the Governor's chancier moves. He had other New Age types in government (such as myself), but they were advisors, consultants, and commission members. State Architect was a line position—highly visible, highly responsible, with an office of 350 to administer and a budget of twelve million dollars to spend (construction budget of $200 million). Legislators, press, and the architectural professionals prepared themselves to ridicule, but they never got a chance.

Sim turned out to be a shockingly good bureaucrat. He had the best press relations of anyone in the administration—thanks to his candor, humor, Dutch good sense, and on-going newsworthiness. His office loved him and did good work, and some of the work was substantial, such as Site One—the largest climate-modulated building yet designed.

Consider the inversion that Sim's success represents. He was a highly effective outlaw of the sixties—involved in the Berkeley People's Park controversy, quit his University of California's professorship to start the alternative technology Farallones Institute. In a mere couple of years, without a public revolution or personal moral compromise, the fringe became the center.

In October 1978, Sim gracefully resigned. What's interesting to me is that by stepping temporarily out of his advocacy role into a policy position, Sim did not diminish his on-going advocacy, but instead strengthened it considerably. Any career advocate might do well by cycling through occasional policy and assistant positions, both in government and business.

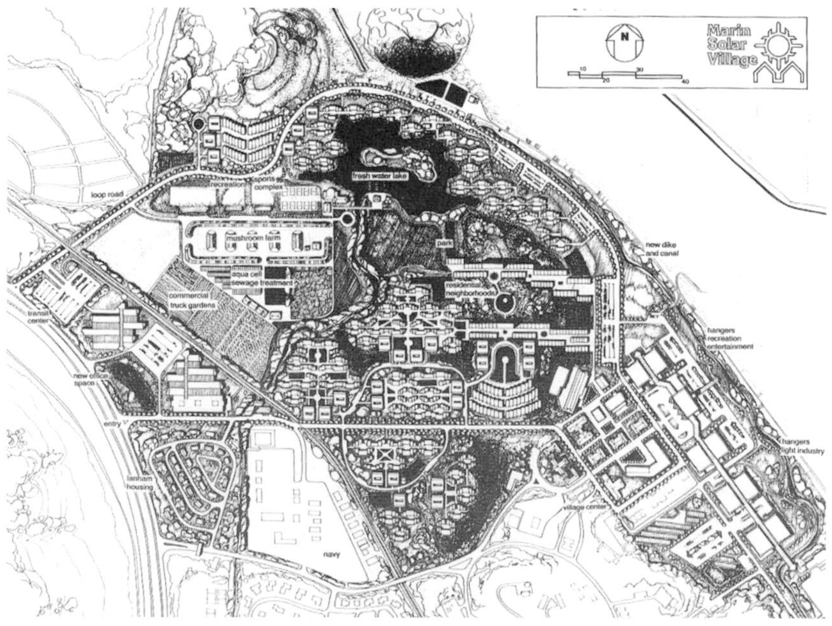

ABOVE
Marin Solar Village model.

LEFT
Marin Solar Village plan.

RIGHT
Marin Solar Village puzzle.

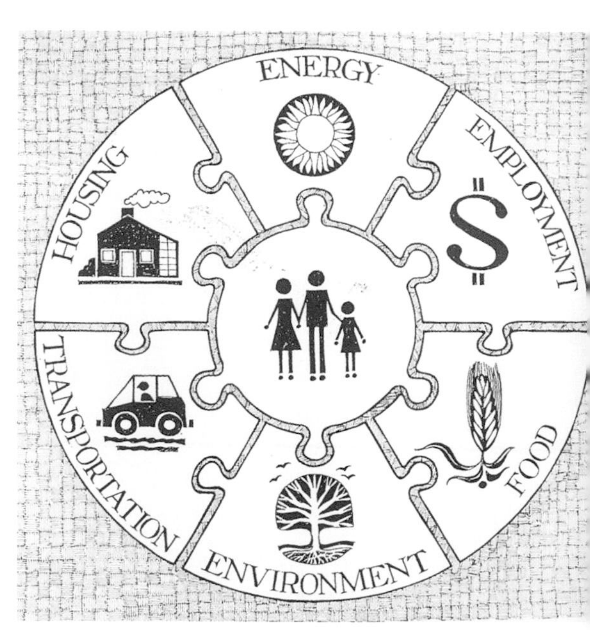

Peter Calthorpe, who had worked with me at Farallones and in Sacramento, convinced me times were ripe to open an architecture and planning practice and to capitalize on the track record we'd racked up in Sacramento. "Okay, Peter, but the office has to be in Inverness. I'll drive to Berkeley two days a week to teach but that's it. You'll have to commute over the hill from San Francisco." Peter, fifteen years younger than I, recognized the opportunity and so we set up shop in one of the three buildings on Inverness's main street.

Soon after returning to Inverness in 1978, the local weekly paper in Marin County, *Pacific Sun,* did a cover-story interview with me in which I talked about extending some of the work we'd done in Sacramento to local communities. I met with the *Sun's* publisher, Steve McNamara, to explore the idea further. Steve and I then met with County Supervisor (now U.S. Senator) Barbara Boxer regarding the future of Hamilton Air Force Base, which had been decommissioned some years earlier. Its location on Highway 101, the major link between San Francisco and the fast-growing suburban corridor to the north, and its large size of over 1,200 acres, including an excellent airstrip and hangars, had developers and enthusiasts for a Marin County airport drooling and environmentalists adamant that the land be open space.

Upon meeting, Barbara said, "Sim, can't you come up with a plan that would satisfy both environmentalists and those people who want affordable housing and a community that demonstrates the things you've been doing in Sacramento such as energy efficiency, more pedestrian-friendly neighborhoods, integrating employment and local services?"

"Let's do at Hamilton all the things you were talking about in your interview. We can have a model community that combines energy-efficient solar homes, centers for local employment, on-site energy and food production, workable mass transit on the old railway line, and return six hundred acres of runway into marsh! And we can get the land for free under the Federal Surplus Property Act, so the whole thing can be affordable. We can satisfy the people who want development and most environmentalists who'd probably be pleased to see a new and better model for development."

That spring I used my design studio at Berkeley to gather the data to begin to develop a plan. A group began forming to support the idea. With Steve McNamara as chairman, we set up a nonprofit corporation, the Marin Solar Village Corporation, and in a relatively short period of time raised $200,000 to do the plan and public education. Much of the money came from the newly formed Federal Solar Energy Research Lab, founded under President Jimmy Carter and headed by Dennis Hayes, the coordinator of the first Earth Day.

With the November election approaching, friends of the Solar Village and interests who supported turning Hamilton into a regional airport for the North Bay were squaring off for a decisive battle regarding the future of Hamilton Air Force Base. Barbara and her allies on the board of supervisors proposed an ordinance that prohibited any county funds from being used for an airport. A second, nonbinding advisory vote, Measure B, was placed on the ballot to solicit support for the Solar Village concept. Two other ballot initiatives called for an airport on the site.

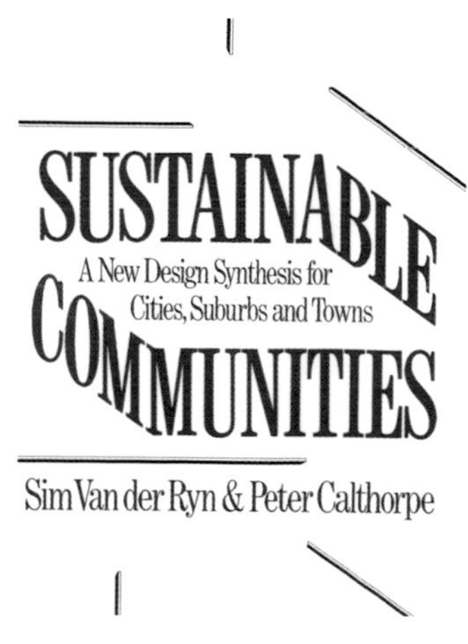

Cover of Sustainable Communities.

Election night we listened to the returns at the *Pacific Sun* office. I, for one, was confident that we would win. We had held meetings all over the county and had a large group of enthusiastic and committed volunteers. The returns started coming in. The pro-airport measures were losing by large margins. The Solar Village Initiative was comfortably ahead. Then the vote from Novato started coming in. Its politicians had been lukewarm toward the Solar Village concept, preferring that nothing happen at the site. At the end of the evening our initiative had failed to get a 50 percent approval by a narrow margin. We were discouraged but not defeated since the vote was nonbinding.

We plunged ahead. We met with Jay Solomon, Director of the General Services Administration (GSA) under President Jimmy Carter and a former developer. We needed GSA approval because a dollar sale to local government was a key to the plan. Solomon was supportive and directed his people to begin the paperwork for a transfer to a Joint City/County Authority to acquire the property for one dollar. We met with Jim Rouse, one of the largest and most progressive community developers in the country, and he expressed his interest in being the master developer for our plan.

A meeting of the Novato/Marin County/Hamilton Joint Powers Authority was set to discuss and vote on whether to enter active negotiations with the Rouse Company on implementing our plan. I made a presentation of the plan. Barbara made a motion to begin negotiations with developers. During my presentation, Solar Village staff were phoning frantically to locate the two Novato representatives—one city council person, one supervisor, who had promised to vote for Barbara's resolution. No one could find them. The vote was called. Marin Solar Village lost by one vote. The plan remained a dream. In 1980, after Reagan's election as president, a republican GSA director rescinded the deal and determined that the base surplus property should be sold at auction to the highest bidder. That began a fifteen-year process that ended when a conventional Bay Area developer was selected to build a largely conventional community. One key environmental feature of the plan survived. The levees are being removed and six hundred acres of concrete runways are being restored as wetlands and habitat for spawning fish and other critters. One step forward.

Marin Solar Village was a dream that affected many people and became the prototype for many positive things that have happened in American urban and regional planning since 1980. Peter Calthorpe, now a leading innovator in urban and regional planning, speaks of the lasting impact of Marin Solar Village: "Sim Van der Ryn planted a seed that has blossomed in many places. For example, many of Marin Solar Village's features are incorporated in the reuse of Denver's former Stapleton Airport where 2,000 acres of riparian corridor replace the former runway. Sim helped show us the way."

"Remembering Solar Village"

By Steve McNamara, Editor, *Pacific Sun*

Sim Van der Ryn's reputation is global, but in Marin he is best known for Marin Solar Village, the nearly successful effort to turn Hamilton Air Force Base into an energy efficient community. The project was supported by President Jimmy Carter's White House, Secretary of the Interior Stewart Udall, the federal Department of Energy, Senator Alan Cranston, Governor Jerry Brown, the head of the state Office of Appropriate Technology, Bill Press and the Marin Board of Supervisors.

So why didn't it happen? Because Hamilton is in Novato and the Novato City Council's support never rose much above lukewarm and then grew markedly chilly.

The idea was hatched one spring day in 1979 at Sim's house in Inverness when I met him to write an article for the *Sun.* At one point the talked turned to sustainable living in an energy efficient community. At another point we talked about the rancorous situation at Hamilton. A group of aviation buffs led by Supervisor Bob Roumiguiere wanted to capture the surplus air base for a commercial airport. Novato officials and residents hated the thought of an airport, but they didn't have an alternate plan.

On that spring day in 1979 Sim and I had another glass or two of wine and then it came to us: why not a sustainable community at Hamilton? It could be a solar village where jobs and housing were matched, where cars were tucked away, gardening encouraged, wastewater handled in an ecological manner and affordable houses built to suit their solar setting. We decided to have a go at it.

The result was an astonishing chapter in Marin's political and environmental history. Sim wrote a massive, inspiring article for the *Sun* entitled, "The Sustainable City," which in its last two paragraphs sprang the idea that an ideal setting for such a city would be Hamilton. I wrote a follow-up editorial saying it was "Time for Vision." Somewhat to our amazement, the idea took off. Friends of Solar Village and then the nonprofit Marin Solar Village Corporation were formed with me as president and Sim as the design brains. Every environmental leader in the county, from Peter Behr and Stewart Brand to Alf Heller and Karin Urquhart, joined the movement. Along with them came literally thousands of residents who saw something idealistic and good they could make happen. Lengthy supportive articles appeared in the *San Francisco Chronicle, San Francisco Examiner, Marin Independent Journal* and the *Bay Guardian.* The Department of Energy awarded us grants of more than sixty thousand dollars for planning and design. Experts in financing and development were brought on board. It was a genuine mass movement.

The deal with Novato was more complicated. Some officials and residents were genuinely supportive. But others saw Solar Village mainly as a handy club with which to beat back the airport forces. The idea itself made them a little nervous. Matching jobs and housing to cut down commuters—wasn't that social engineering?

Differences were put aside during two thunderous countywide elections pitting Solar Village against airport backers. The results were mixed—neither side's ballot measures gained a majority, although Solar Village did better than the airport.
So the airport was dead and it was time to push harder for Solar Village. Most of the politicians were willing—those from the White House on down to the Marin Board of Supervisors.

But the Novato City Council had contracted a case of cold feet. At a joint meeting of the supervisors and Novato council in January 1981, Marin Solar Village died a testy death. It was a four-to-one vote in favor by the supervisors and a two-to-two tie vote by Novato. (Councilwoman Susan Stompe was missing.) Both groups had needed to approve it, and so after a tumultuous twenty-two months the dream was snuffed out.

CLIMATE RESPONSIVE DESIGN STRATEGIES

COLD DAY HEATING MODE

A. The mass of the highly insulated straw bale and PISE walls produces a thermal "flywheel" effect, storing and releasing heat.

B. Stored heat in the thermal mass in the concrete floor and columns is also released to help maintain comfort.

C. Efficient wood-burning stoves (working display models) are the only source of supplemental heat.

D. Lightshelves control glare and direct gain, reflecting light onto the curved ceiling.

E. Doors and windows can be opened to provide immediate cooling if the temperature indoors is too warm.

F. The low winter sun penetrates the building through substantial south-facing glazing.

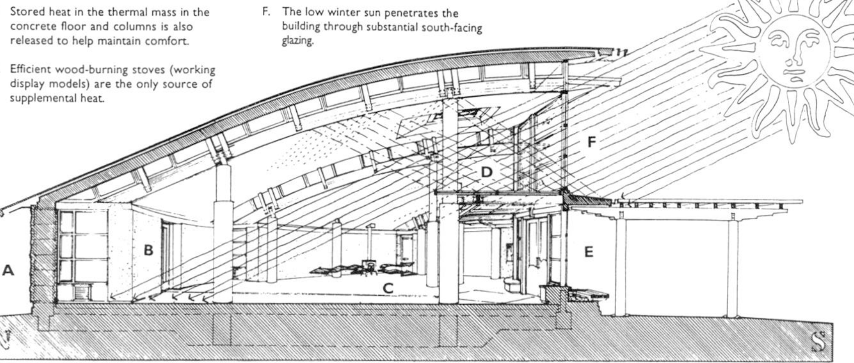

HOT DAY COOLING MODE

A. The thermal mass and high insulation value of the straw bale and PISE (sprayed soil-cement) walls protect against the transfer of 100°F plus outdoor summer temperatures.

B. Air space in the roof ventilates heat from the radiant barrier over 12" of cellulose insulation (R-60).

C. Clerestory windows are closed when the outside temperature exceeds the interior temperature.

D. A white synthetic rubber roof membrane reflects gain from solar radiation.

E. The thermal mass of the concrete floor and columns absorb heat from people and equipment and stores "coolth" from the previous night flush.

F. Overhang and awnings shade windows, controlling solar gain. Light shelves and a curved white ceiling distribute daylight evenly, reducing the need for heat-producing lighting fixtures.

G. Planted trellis shades walls, windows,, and walkway in summer; allows solar gain in winter; and controls glare.

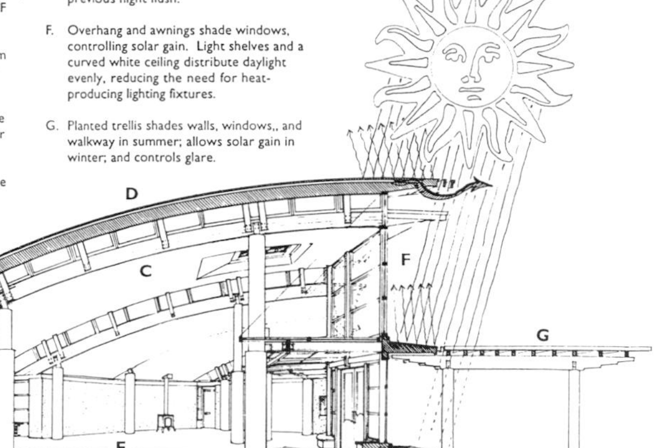

NIGHT HEATING MODE

A. The insulation in the straw bale walls and roof helps retain the day's heat in side the building mass.

B. The 12" cellulose (recycled newspaper) insulation in the roof provides an R-value greater than 60.

C. The wood-burning stoves can be left on a slow burn on the coldest nights, balancing heat loss.

D. Lightshelves are hinged can be folded against the high glazing to reduce heat loss to the night sky.

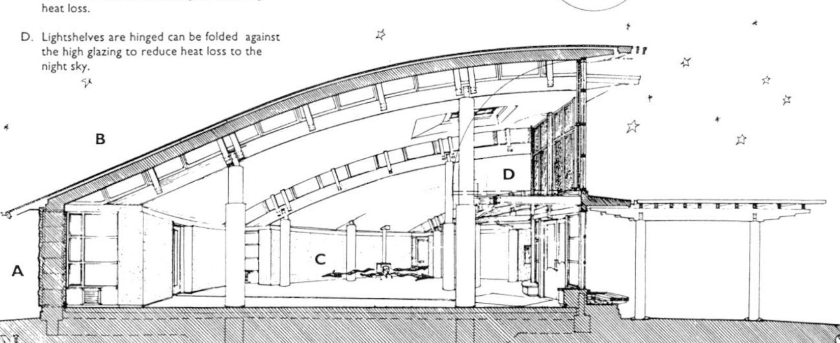

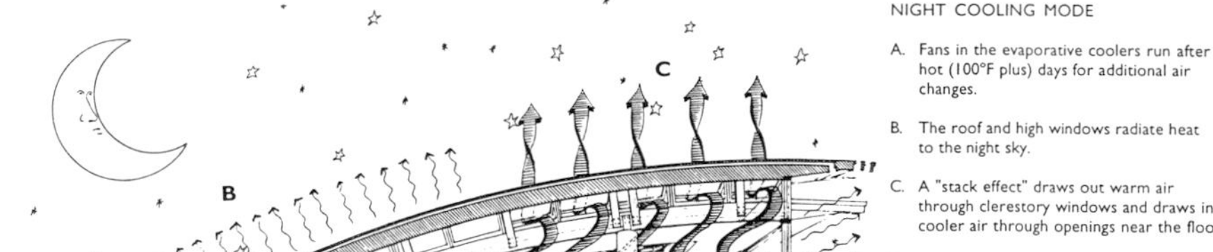

NIGHT COOLING MODE

A. Fans in the evaporative coolers run after hot (100°F plus) days for additional air changes.

B. The roof and high windows radiate heat to the night sky.

C. A "stack effect" draws out warm air through clerestory windows and draws in cooler air through openings near the floor.

D. Night sky radiation and cool night temperatures are used to "charge" the thermal mass of the building with "coolth" for the next day.

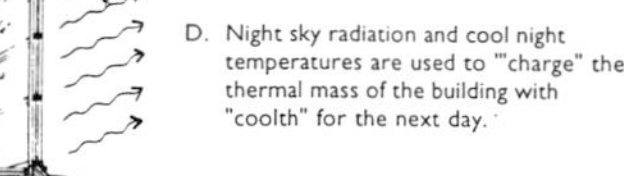

Real Goods Climate Responsive Design Strategies.

real goods solar living center

After retiring from UC Berkeley in 1995 and making the commitment to full-time architectural practice, I didn't have to wait long for the right project to come along. Real Goods Trading Company was founded to supply back-to-the-landers in northern California with technology appropriate to a resourceful rural lifestyle. By the mid-nineteen nineties, it had grown into a national mail order company, the largest supplier of solar living products and solar electric systems in the country. Its founder and president, John Schaeffer, is a visionary and a smart businessman.

The company was outgrowing its headquarters, a cluster of anonymous metal buildings in the industrial area of Ukiah, a small city two hours north of San Francisco. John purchased a twelve-acre site in Hopland, a crossroads and a wine grape-growing town fifteen minutes south of Ukiah. The site, once agricultural, had been used as a highway department dump site. It was bordered by Highway 101, Feliz Creek, a tributary to the Russian River, which drains the northern interior to the coast, and an old logging railroad.

John's vision was to transform this ecologically wounded site into a model of ecological restoration, demonstration gardens, and outdoor people space, and as the centerpiece, build a showroom that would be a model of sustainable design practices. His brief for the project states that Real Goods wants a building that "takes less from the Earth and gives back more to people." He wanted to create a building that uses no outside energy sources, uses locally available environmentally benign materials, recycles wastes generated by its occupants, and restores the badly damaged site to full biological productivity.

Real Goods invited six architects to compete in preparing concept plans for the proposed Solar Living Center. I found John's vision statement for the project so closely aligned with my own values that I gladly accepted the invitation.

Together with David Arkin, a talented and experienced architect who had joined my firm, I spent a day on the barren site. Pulling out my ever-present watercolor kit, I sat quietly on the railroad bridge, letting the site speak to me through my eyes and hands as I sketched. The process is my form of meditation: a way to get quiet and become aware of the subtleties of place, light, colors, forms and patterns, sounds, and spaces. Watercolor painting helps me to experience an environment fully with my whole being. It's the difference between looking, which is passive involvement, and seeing, which is active engagement with place.

Sim beginning design with a day of watercolor on the Real Goods site.

After painting, I started sketching. The topographic map we were given showed a slight mound at the south end of the site. The highest point, offering protection from flooding, was where the building should be. Sitting there for several hours, the highway noise became increasingly irritating. Why not scoop out part of the site to create ponds and water elements that John's brief mentioned and use the material to create a berm, or earth mound, to screen the building from the highway noise and view? If the Center was to be the oasis that John referred to in his brief, then it should not be like most highway commercial development that insists it be visible from the road. Instead we could hide it and create a series of ecological cues announcing that something interesting was around the bend. As part of that theme, I sketched an entrance road alongside the creek corridor, which would be restored. Instead of parking being the first thing you saw, the visitor would have time to take several breaths, leave the highway behind, park in the back, and enter another reality.

ABOVE
Flow forms fed by solar pump from recycled redwood tank.

Inside the rounded berm, I sketched the building as a south-facing curve. Why not make the building truly invisible and adapted to the hot summers by using a sod roof, arbors to shade the south wall, and a thick wall built into the berm on the north where the winter winds came from? Why not have the building open onto a central meeting space marked by a shallow round pond that could provide cooling in summer? To the north, I located the experimental gardens and orchards mentioned in John's program.

I went home and that weekend, David and I developed the competition drawings based on my sketches. As another meditation, I spent a day carefully doing the finished drawings and sent the package off to Real Goods. We later went up and presented it and answered questions. And then, as is common in the architecture business, we waited and then waited some more. Finally I heard from John, "Congratulations! You got the job!"

I added structural engineer Bruce King, and graduate student Adam Jackaway, a specialist in climate adaptive strategies, to the team. Real Goods added landscape designers Stephanie Kotin and Chris Tebbut and project manager Jeff Oldham. Collectively, we made the decision to reverse the usual design process, where the landscaping is the last element to be installed in a project. "Why not put in the landscape first and give it a year to get established before you start construction?" Chris exclaimed. And that's what happened. Chris and Stephanie, besides being inspired designers, are hands-on horticulturists and readers of the land. The key fact is that the site is a floodplain, and as Chris and Stephanie explained, floodplains are highly diverse ecosystems. The trees and plants they chose were all adapted to flooding conditions.

Their concept received its first test soon after they completed planting when a flood in 1995 put the site under four feet of water. All the plantings survived and, indeed, have prospered. Their landscape plan builds in various solar clocks that mark the cycle of seasons and the cardinal directions. We integrated our ideas that the site should tell a sun story, a water story, a native plant restoration story, and a food plant story. The stories are built into the design, and it's interesting to watch visitors with no prior knowledge discover for themselves what stories the place has to tell.

There were also unexpected interactions among the stories that I hadn't anticipated. As a visitor enters the center area, a large recycled redwood wine tank spills water over its top into a flow-form stream below, starting the water story. The tank is filled from the ponds at the end of the water story by a solar powered pump. When the sun is full force, the water volume is at a peak. When a cloud drifts by and obscures the sun, flow from the pump drops and the sound of water, designed to mask highway noise, diminishes. I've watched people walk by the stream when this occurs, look around them, and slowly make the connection between the sun and the water flow.

My competition sketch for the building plan started to adapt to new information and reality. The idea of a heavy earth-covered roof would require a massive structure that would interfere with Real Goods' desire for open floor space. Adam suggested a curved roof and light shelf that would bounce daylight off the curved roof for very even light distribution. We liked the idea, constructed a model, and tested it in a heliodyne, a device that simulates sun path for any location. The setup included a tiny video camera that gave us a recording of sun and shade patterns within the model for the lowest and highest sun angles—the winter and summer solstices—and also for the fall and spring equinoxes. John Schaeffer was worried that the curved roof would cost more than a flat roof. We went up to his office and ran the ten-minute time-lapse video showing the actual light inside the building. It sold him on our idea.

Our working method was collaboration. The level of integration we achieved in the building and site design was possible only by eroding the traditional professional boundaries in both design and construction. And it was more fun. Our working method related project goals to the five principles of ecological design articulated in my book:

Ecological Design:
Goal 1: Create a Climate Responsive Building (Solutions Grow from Place)
Goal 2: Create an Educational Environment (Make Nature Visible)
Goal 3: Design for Low Impact Construction (Ecologic Accounting Informs Design)
Goal 4: Involve Everyone and Have Fun (Everyone is a Designer)

ABOVE
Real Goods strawbale shed.

BOTTOM
Real Goods pond.

RIGHT
Real Goods Solar Living Center.

FACING
Real Goods Solar Living Center. Charles C. Benton, Kite Aerial Photography.

RIGHT
Curved Roof of western facade.

FACING
Open floor space

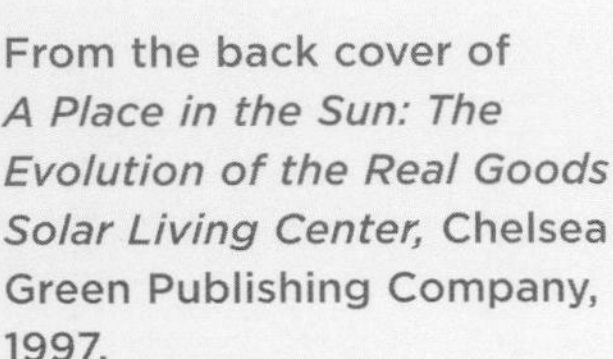
From the back cover of *A Place in the Sun: The Evolution of the Real Goods Solar Living Center,* Chelsea Green Publishing Company, 1997.

The Real Goods Solar Living Center, which opened in Hopland, California, in June 1996, embodies the building materials, landscaping techniques, renewable energy technologies, and human design processes that future generations will take for granted. Its massive earth-covered walls built of straw bales, whimsical "living structures," an automobile graveyard where trees "drive-through" cars (for a change) and the nation's largest solar calendar, have already surprised and delighted many thousands of visitors.

"A truly magical and inspirational place."

"Overwhelming and thought provoking—just really cool!"

—Comments from the guest register at the Solar Living Center

With the project management team of David Arkin and Jeff Oldham, the design seemed to get better every day. Finally we went out to bid, as required by the bank loan. I had argued that this unusual building required a negotiated bid. The company accepted the low bid of a conventional commercial contractor. I spent a sleepless night worrying that it couldn't be built for this bid, and we were in for trouble. Then I had an idea: in initiating the project, let's do a day of education where the contractor, his superintendent, and foreman for all the trades, gather on-site and we explain the design, how and why it is the way it is, with models and drawings, and answer all of their questions. That project orientation day and its follow-up made the difference. Architectural training and practice is largely cut off from the people who really do the work, from the people who, as one architect said to me, "are just robots with nail guns." Bringing everyone into the design and its rationale made them feel they were part of something bigger and more important than simply working on another job. They became invested in our ideas and found ways to improve on them.

I now use this process wherever I can in initiating construction, embracing the people who are responsible for making my drawings into buildings, and sharing my "whys" and "hows" through a tour of the design process and design decisions. In earlier times, design and construction were not divided. The master builders and master designers who toiled hundreds of years on the cathedrals shared the same vision. Architect Richard Fernau puts it this way, "I've always thought of architecture as a kind of philosophic carpentry. It's very much the Zen idea—you don't find truth through precepts or concepts, you find it through doing. And from there you can learn something larger."

The Solar Living Center, although several hours from a major urban center, attracts hundreds of thousands of visitors each year. Last year's Annual Solfest brought twenty thousand people to the site. It's a success story of an owner with a clear vision, an architect who got it, a collaborative team that made it happen, and a public that loves it.

ABOVE
Guitar House, aerial view.

RIGHT
Guitar House, exploded view watercolor.

FAR RIGHT
Guitar House, entry.

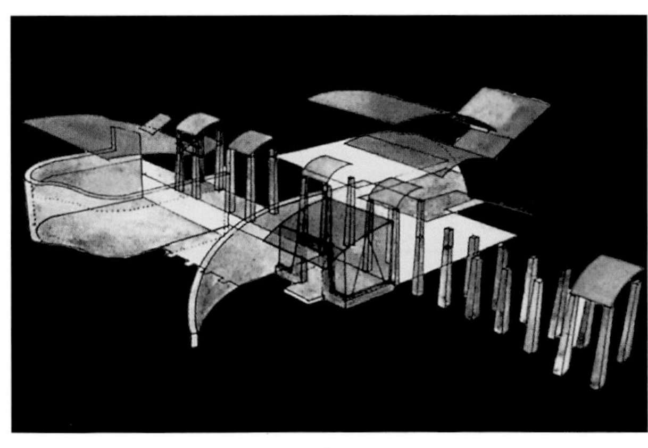

ABOVE
Interior staircase, Red Rock Retreat, Torrey, Utah.

LEFT
Red Rock Retreat, Torrey, Utah. Photograph © Libby Dietrich.

a tale of two houses

This is a story of two homes. What is similar about them is that both are green in their approach to design, both were designed by me, both are happily lived in by satisfied clients. Everything else is very different. One is on a secluded hilltop in the San Francisco Bay area; the other is in the red rock country of central Utah. One house is very large, the other very modest. One house involved inventing new construction techniques involving close, continuous, and complex cooperation for more than five years between our design team, a highly skilled construction team, and the client. The other home was designed on-site in three days with the clients and a visit from their contractor, and built by him from my hand-drawn plans in a matter of months.

the guitar house

We called it the Guitar House because the long east-west gallery with its forty rammed-earth columns looks like the neck and frets of a guitar, while the music room at the end of the corridor is shaped like the body of the guitar. It has windows, each one a note, and together they form a chord from Jerry Garcia's tune, "Friend of the Devil." The client is a skilled amateur musician, a successful entrepreneur, and a formidable and highly effective champion of environmental causes.

My client had purchased a ridge top, wooded, sixteen-acre estate overlooking San Francisco. The existing house on the property was unremarkable in its design. The client wanted to build a home that, while large, would incorporate his environmental principles. Upon moving there, he established a large organic garden and greenhouse. I told him that in our northern California Mediterranean climate we could design a passive solar home that regulated its interior temperature naturally, and like the Real Goods Solar Living Center, generated all its own electricity from the sun. Although connected to the city sewer, we also designed it so wastewater could flow into a constructed wetland water garden that would process the effluent biologically.

He wanted to use as little wood as possible in his home, and whatever wood was required would have to be reclaimed from existing buildings or certified as harvested from responsibly managed forests. The major building technique we settled on was rammed earth and its counterpart, sprayed earth. I had experience with rammed earth at Farallones Institute where, with a UC design class, we constructed a garden building in rammed earth, guided by David Easton, a pioneer in reintroducing this ancient building technique to the United States. The process was fun: build forms, pour in waste low-grade non-expansive soils mixed with some cement and very little water, and compact it with pneumatic tampers. The result of our Farallones experiment in the 1980s was a rough, uneven finish. My client wanted a very smooth, almost stone-like finish. This meant we would need forms with a very smooth interior and very sturdy bracing that would not vibrate or move during the intense pressure of pneumatic compacting.

I recommended Dave Warner's company, Redhorse Constructors, to be the builder. I had worked with Dave before and knew him as a high-energy builder with strong environmental values and an enthusiasm for taking on challenging projects. We located a beautiful reddish tone quarry waste in nearby Napa and began building test columns in the contractor's corporate yard. The column form started as an octagon and ended up as a square on top with four rectangular sides and four triangular sides. To make things still more complex, I drew a profile of the whole gallery of columns and then drew an imaginary geologic strata through them. This meant each column had to use three different color mixes to carefully calibrated points. In addition, we wanted to replace as much of the cement as possible with flyash, a waste by-product of coal-fired power plants.

FACING LEFT
Guitar House, interior hallway.

FACING RIGHT
Guitar House, view from the entry pathway.

Rammed earth is an unfamiliar technique for most building departments. To obtain building permits requires peer reviews by one, and in our case, two engineering firms with rammed earth experience. We decided not to wait for complete plans before we began construction. Instead we built the garage first using the basic vocabulary of sprayed earth walls, rammed columns, and curved zinc roofs as a test of the construction techniques while we moved forward with the complete design of the whole house.

While the basic design of the house did not change from the idea of a strong east-west sun-capturing colonnade with rooms attached, the configuration and size underwent many transformations, growing steadily larger to three times the initial plan. The client's life and interests were changing and were reflected in changing design. The long, continuous design and construction period was like birthing and bringing up a child, where everyday something new happens.

The all-star team of craftsmen working on the house was amazing. They knew this was a once-in-a-lifetime opportunity to build something of great durability, beauty, and craftsmanship, and they gave it everything they had. The same crew labored together for more than five years. Details were drawn and redrawn. Mock-ups of innovative systems were built and tested. We began a program of testing the strength of the rammed earth, which continued for five years, showing that unlike concrete, which attains its final strength in several months, the compressive strength of the rammed earth continued to increase every year.

Natural light creates interior architecture. Light spills out from skylight towers along the gallery, from massive shaded sliding doors on the south, and from the private deck above. The natural earth and stone colors glow with reflected light. Little furniture or decoration is needed for one to feel at home and sheltered within. I like to design with curves, and the guitar house is composed of complex curves, giving it the feeling and energy of a living body.

My only wish is that more people could actually visit this place to experience innovative green technology and construction techniques. The house is married to its site, boasts superb lasting craftsmanship, has a sense of peace and permanence, and boasts a design that is neither traditional, nor modernist or showy. Just right.

LEFT
Removing rammed-earth column formwork at Guitar House. Courtesy of Redhorse Constructors.

BELOW
Spraying gun earth at Guitar House. Courtesy of Redhorse Constructors.

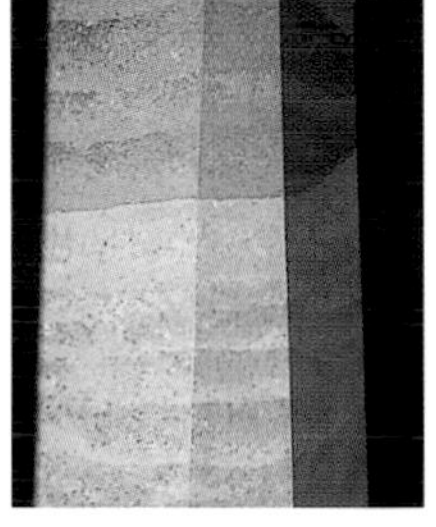

ABOVE
Detail of colonnade.

FACING
Guitar House, rammed-earth colonnade entryway.

red rock retreat

In the fall of 2001, Libby Dietrich, a Sausalito-based consultant, contacted me. She and her husband had purchased a site in Torrey, Utah, in the beautiful red rock country and wanted to plan a home there. They had spent considerable time camping on the site. I asked them to send me notes and ideas regarding what they wanted in a house, and was impressed by the clarity and directness of their thinking. They knew what they wanted and were able to communicate it clearly. Many clients come in with hundreds of pictures collected from design magazines, but I prefer to begin with a clear written statement describing spaces, activities, budget, and feeling. Too many magazine clips start to cancel each other out and only confuse. We agreed on a date between Christmas and New Year's when I would spend three days with them on-site to help plan the house. I told them that should be enough time for me to translate their ideas into a workable plan.

I drove five hours from the Salt Lake City airport to Torrey, near Capitol Reef National Park. The next morning, we went out to their site on a bluff overlooking a river valley. They wanted a simple house that worked with local materials, site, and climate with its summer and winter extremes. David, a former law professor, is partially disabled by a stroke, which leaves him with an active, engaging mind and presence but impaired speech. He knew exactly what views were most important to him from his favorite chair. After visiting the site, we spent some time sketching. When we had a rough plan sketch, we went back with stakes and layout tape to see how it fit the site. We walked through the rooms and made various adjustments. Later, I began to do a measured pencil drawing of the two-story floor plan and building section.

They had found local builder David Moosman to work with. I always ask clients to select a contractor early in the design process. This is particularly important when I'm designing away from my home location. Using local knowledge is critical to successful projects. Moosman, a man who wasted no words, reviewed the sketches and made suggestions about materials and systems. We wanted to use the local red rock, which is everywhere, for a major element. We decided on stucco with a similar color. In this location, a large sheltered porch with shade trellises extends the usable indoor space during the warmer months, and so this was added. With his builder's transit, we checked ground elevations to make sure the home would site on the land without intruding. We had moved it to the edge of the bluff, incorporating David's favorite views. I suggested that actual window locations be determined when the house was framed.

In many areas, the "soft" costs of preparing full architectural and engineering plans, going through local design review and planning approvals, permit fees, and special assessments can add thirty percent or more to the cost of a home project. In Torrey, no planning or building permits are required. I'm not advocating we do away with planning and building regulation; however, many localities simply have too many cumbersome rules and regulations. Libby and David had a retired architect draw up two sheets of plans with some revisions. Moosman went to work. Unlike most projects where there are phone calls, faxes, and e-mails flying around among client, architect, and builder, in this case there were none.

What Libby and David got was a well-built and crafted 1,200-square-foot house, not including extensive decks and trellising, for a cost of $100 per square foot. I wish that an architect's life were always this simple and satisfying without all the bureaucratic, legalistic, risk-averse elements of our business, which add costs and destroy creativity and common sense.

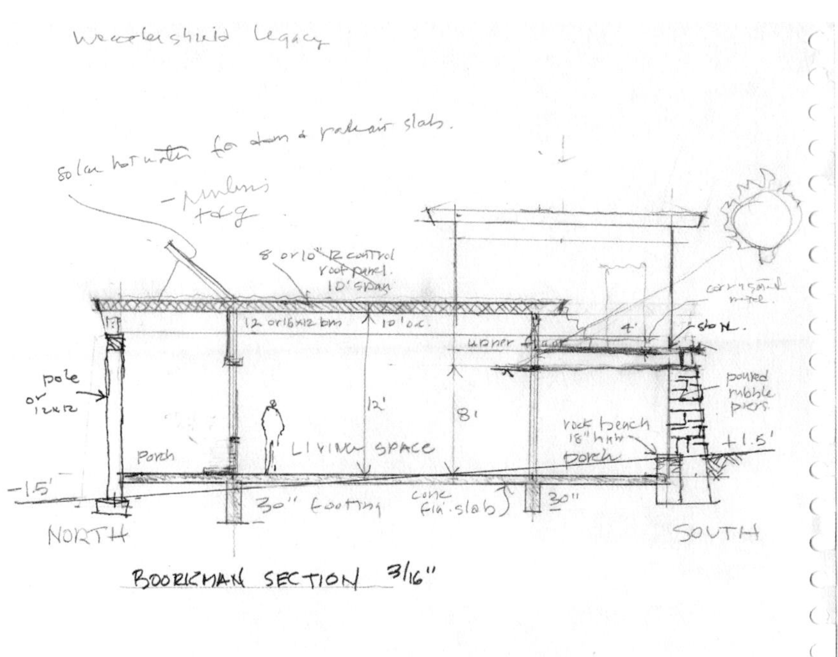

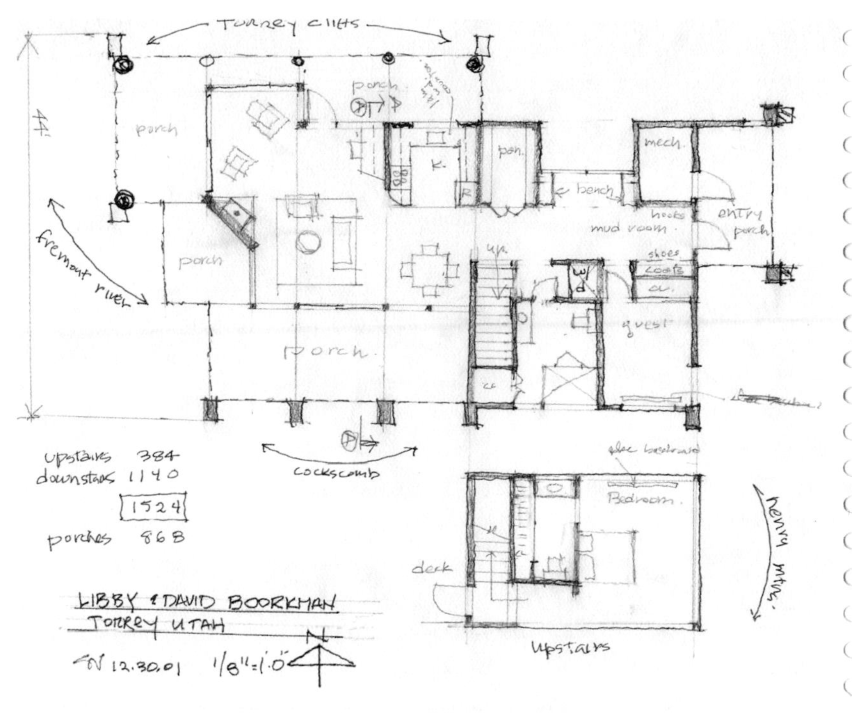

ABOVE LEFT and RIGHT
Red Rock Retreat, sketch and diagram.

LEFT
Red Rock Retreat, Torrey, Utah.

a tale of two institutions

Over the years, we have learned what it takes to make a building that is green and follows ecological principles. First of all, you need a client who understands and is committed to creating and funding an environmental building. Then you need a design process that allows this to happen. This means active client participation and engagement in the process. It means collaboration not only between architect and client but also from the earliest stages, including all the other key disciplines involved, such as the builder, structural and mechanical engineer, and other consultants, depending on the project.

Accomplishing results can become difficult with corporate, government, or other institutional clients who are organized on hierarchical bureaucratic models, follow linear sequential planning models, and have highly compartmentalized roles, responsibilities, and value structures. The usual organizational model tends to avoid risk and innovation. Indeed, risk-taking innovation and exceptional results may be actively discouraged as rocking the boat.

This is the story of our experience on two college campuses. One is a community college in California, the other a highly unusual four-year-college in rural Kentucky. In both cases the client wanted a green building, but the process and the results were very different.

de anza college

De Anza College in Cupertino, California, is a two-year college in the heart of Silicon Valley. A group of De Anza College faculty, staff, and students spent nine years envisioning a new environmental science center combining interdisciplinary studies, energy management, and distance learning. They also envisioned it as a gathering place for community and business functions. The group succeeded in securing a site on the campus master plan, on derelict paving adjacent to the campus native plant demonstration oasis. The new project is a model of practical climate responsive design, including a photovoltaic system for on-site electrical production.

When the group interviewed us as the prospective architects, we said that we felt they weren't quite ready yet for a building design. We proposed first a series of open workshops to explore and document what the project's goals were and to provide them graphic materials for fund-raising. The group jumped at the idea. They made the connection that the living building they dreamed of needed a living design process. The college was planning a $250 million bond issue for new facilities, including the Environmental Studies Building. However, there was no money available for the crucial visioning work. Julie Phillips, the chairperson of Environmental Studies, and Don Aitken, a long-time solar advocate and advisor to the program, convinced the student government to put up the money for us to design and implement a collaborative process with them. This was great news, although there was one person who was unhappy about it: the facilities director for the district. He maintained tight control over the entire design and construction process and he was hostile towards the collaborative design process we were proposing.

We proposed four workshops. The group publicized them widely, both on the campus and on the Internet. Since De Anza College is a commuter campus, the extra efforts to encourage participation were especially important. Our goal was to assemble everyone interested and to provide a forum for all ideas and critiques to be heard.

Rendering of the Kirsch Center at De Anza College, Cupertino, California.

The first workshop was an open forum for listening to and recording ideas. Everyone had a chance to be heard. The core group members provided site constraint information and programming wish lists. Students, faculty, and staff poured out ideas.

This session was particularly productive. We organized it in a formal brainstorming format, listing a series of topics on big pads of newsprint. As the ideas flew we recorded every one without judgment. The power of this technique is that inhibitions dissolve, and a wonderful collection of phases emerged before us, ranging from the goals of the project to specific building techniques. Most importantly, everyone attending felt heard and respected.

At the next session everyone met at the site. We observed and recorded important site relationships and their connections to the flow of human activities. Most importantly, we all felt a growing sense of common purpose. Back at the meeting room, we pored over the lists from the first session. Together we built consensus for the most important features of the project. By the end of the session we were sketching the first ruminations of the building's form with the group.

For the third session we presented a set of rough concept drawings to prime the discussion, but *we didn't start with those drawings.* We started with a *site plan* showing the constraints and opportunities of the specific site. Then, on layer after layer of tracing paper, we sketched what the group had asked for. It was obvious to everyone that the emerging design grew directly out of their criteria. The atmosphere in the room was electric with excitement. A student representative exclaimed, "This makes all the meetings in my years of student government worth it!" We marked the group's ideas for changes directly on the drawings. Later the group met on its own and sent additional ideas for changes.

The final session included our engineers and cost estimator. It's unusual to include them this early in the design process, but their perspectives are essential for getting a project off to a solid start, and the group appreciated their inclusion. We presented the updated design drawings as we did earlier, sketching the group's requests and showing how the design grew out of those requests. At the end of the session the group enthusiastically asked us to prepare a booklet summarizing their criteria and showing some of the design drawings.

The resulting publication was instrumental in raising a two-million-dollar gift from Steve Kirsch, a Silicon Valley entrepreneur. Then a long, multiyear process of behind-the-scenes tug-of-war began with the facilities director, who wielded considerable power with the district board. The building had to be scaled down, and we had to fight and justify every green feature, not once but many times. Only through the persistence and political adroitness of Environmental Studies Chair Julie Phillips and her staff did we prevail and finally break ground in February 2004.

berea college

Berea College is in Berea, Kentucky, a small town that sits where the bluegrass meets the hills of Appalachia. It was founded by Presbyterian ministers as a school for runaway slaves in 1855. Berea's founders held fast to their vision of a college and a community committed to interracial education, to the Appalachian region, and to the equality of women and men from all "nations and climes." Today Berea has a diverse student body, all of whom are on full scholarships, and most from Appalachia. They not only take classes, but also work in various jobs for the college.

A new president came to Berea in 1994: Larry Shinn, a religion scholar formerly at Oberlin College. While at Oberlin, Larry had built a passive solar home for his family, no small feat in the southern Ohio climate. He announced a goal for Berea's campus: "Let's remodel and build new buildings designed so that our campus is carbon neutral in terms of its operations by 2020."

The campus has a coal-fired plant that generates heat for its buildings. Rocky Mountain Institute, a leading nonprofit organization developing resource-efficient solutions, and Ove Arup, an internationally respected advanced engineering firm, were retained to develop campus-wide energy. Van der Ryn Architects was retained to remodel the main academic building, the seventy-year-old, three-story Draper Hall.

ABOVE
Draper Hall Hallway before the renovation.

LEFT
The Draper Hall renovation included a new atrium and skylight for natural daylight and ventilation.

Later, we were retained to design an Ecovillage, which would include family housing, a demonstration sustainable house, and a child development center on a single site. Both projects began with a programming and design workshop, or charette. The Ecovillage charette involved thirty-five Berea staff, students, and faculty participants and four members of the Van der Ryn Architects team. Berea, unlike many colleges, is a true community of faculty, students, and administrators. The group spent an intense day and a half developing qualitative and quantitative criteria for the building renovation.

A working group developed a facilities program for the site and presented it to the larger group, along with a discussion of the opportunities and constraints presented by the site. The group broke up into four subgroups who, each working with someone from Van der Ryn Architects, developed diagrammatic master plans for the site. Each group focused on a particular set of concerns or overlay: social ecology, building ecology, and site ecology. After Van der Ryn Architects presented criteria relating to environmental and social goals, the work groups reformed and continued with further master plan sketches. At the end of the first day, the entire group reviewed each of the four plans. The morning of the second day included a presentation by the architects on vernacular vocabularies for construction, a shared goal for the project. The teams then went to work refining the four proposals, with an emphasis on working towards consensus on a single master plan. After a few intense hours, the group agreed on a single sketch, which remained largely intact in the finished project.

LEFT
Sim Van der Ryn works with staff and students at Berea College in a charette break-out group in the early stages of Ecovillage design

FACING TOP LEFT
Completed Berea College Ecovillage housing and SENS house.

FACING TOP RIGHT
Van der Ryn Architect's' rendering of Ecovillage housing.

FACING BOTTOM
Van der Ryn Architects' aerial rendering of Ecovillage housing.

designing the design process

The examples of our experience at De Anza and Berea colleges and other institutions suggest that if we are to create green campuses and other institutions, we need strategies that change the conventional institutional design process. Greening schools and campuses is a high priority for two reasons. First, they make up a huge block of total construction and have a big impact on overall energy and material use. Second, students spend a significant amount of their days—twelve to twenty years—in school buildings. Making the design, operation, and improvement of their buildings part of curriculum could create a revolution in what and how students learn. They are the ones who are going to have to live with and solve the mess the last generations have created. We need to give them real-life models and experiences that offer alternatives to the conventional processes and products.

First, let's take a look at the typical institutional design process:

RIGHT
Institutional Design Process, watercolor diagram.

Anatomy of the Institutional Design Process

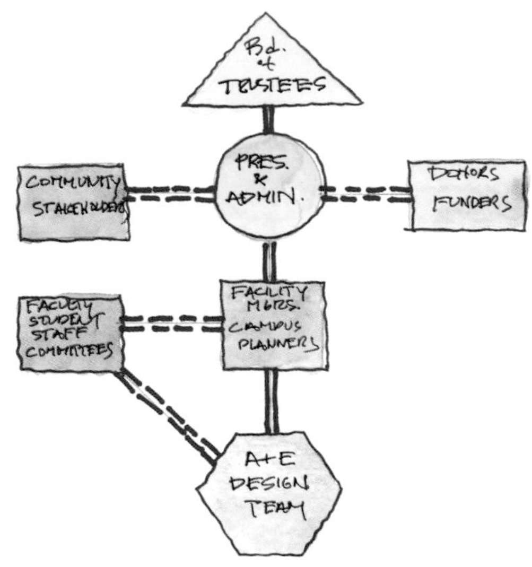

This diagram shows the roles and connections among the players in the usual campus development process. At the center is the administration, the decision takers. They are responsible to a board of trustees whose role is to set policy and review administrative decisions. Building planning, design, and operations is the domain of facilities managers reporting to the president. Once a project has been approved by trustees and the top administrative officer, facilities managers are the implementers, the decision shapers. The architectural, engineering, and construction team selected to carry out the project generally reports to the facilities manager. Community stakeholders, or influential donors and funders, may influence top administrative decisions, while faculty/student/staff committees selected to give input to the project often represent building users. Although these committees may influence the process and its outcome, their role is usually advisory.

This command and control model may work more or less well, depending on whether or not the values of the important players in the game are explicit and well understood.

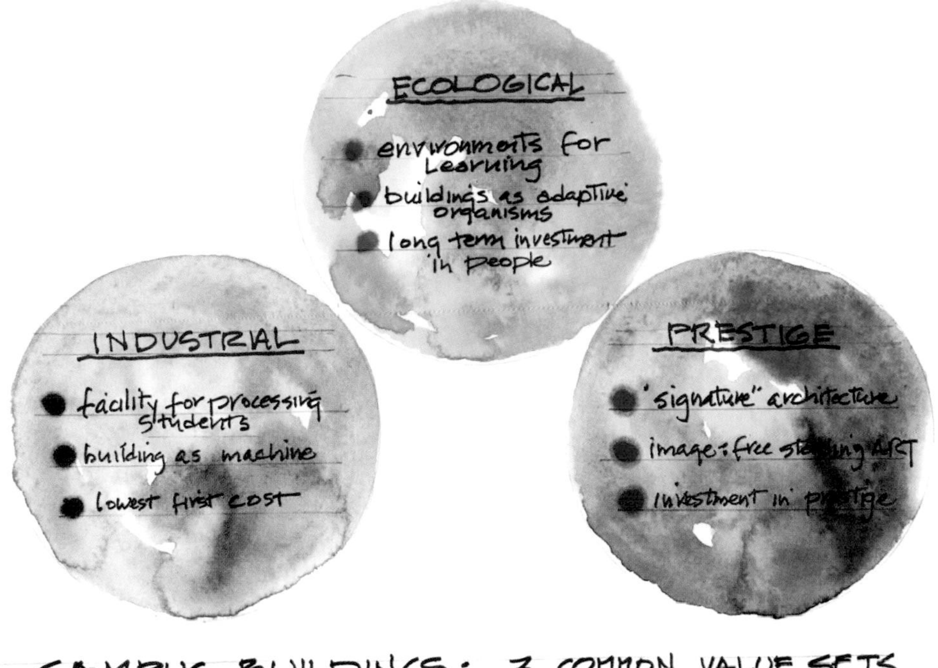

The three dominant value sets that rule institutional design.

Institutional design is ruled by one or more of three dominant sets of values:

Industrial

- Building as machine for processing people (students)
- Lowest first cost

Prestige

- Building as image
- Signature architecture
- Investment in prestige

Ecological

- Environments for learning
- Buildings as adaptive organisms
- Long-term investment in people and facility

The *Industrial* value set is still the most common, certainly for public education at all levels. The *Prestige* value set is common for institutions that are considered prestigious, or for trustees or major donors who value prestige. The third set, *Ecological,* has only been visible in the last fifteen years. Its visibility has been enhanced by the U.S. Green Building Council's LEED Green Building Rating System, where a building's "greenness" is rated using a point system with designations from Platinum to Certified, depending on the building's score. LEED has increased awareness in the corporate and institutional worlds of the benefits of green buildings and, by creating a rating system, provides the incentive of a high-scoring green building as a mark of prestige. The standard design process is set up to produce buildings that follow the industrial model. As we learned at De Anza College, it is not easy to get to green values using that model.

players in the process and their goals

There are various goals at play in the design process. The first two are the simple metrics of *first cost* and *schedule*. The third is more a complex variable: *building performance*. First cost is easy to measure, but performance is far more complex. First, we must assess if the building's mission or program is spelled out qualitatively as well as in the usual square foot numbers and space relationships. We must also take into account accepted measures of greenness, such as energy efficiency, measures of consumption, and emissions of fossil fuels, water, and electricity. Building performance can also include harder-to-measure aspects such as adaptability to future changes of use. The most difficult aspect of performance to gauge is the effect the building has on human productivity, health, and well-being. Post-occupancy evaluation (POE) could give us objective metrics, but thirty years after the invention of POE, the practice of a science of building ecology is just emerging. Building performance implies quantitative and qualitative measures, some easy to gauge—such as operating costs per year—others more difficult, such as what contribution the building makes towards learning.

The diagram shows a pie chart for each of the roles in the design process, assigning a relative value that each role might give to each of the three goals. The decision approvers (trustees) tend to value cost and performance equally. Performance might include values such as prestige and image, an innovative use, or as is increasingly true, a LEED Gold-Rated building. The decision takers (administration) have to balance all interests. Performance, cost, and schedule are all equally important. The facilities manager tends to be focused on two issues: cost and schedule. Aspects of performance may be sacrificed to meet the demands for a predictable schedule and a controlled budget. The other players who influence the process, the campus community and the larger community, are primarily concerned with how the building will meet their needs and interests. Cost and schedule are not their problems.

The political and process dynamic lays in how the design process resolves differences between the values and goals that different players attach to the project. When it comes to the conflicts between interests that typically surface in the standard design process, the saying goes, "You've got three goals, and you only get to pick two."

I have gone into this detail on how the typical hierarchical

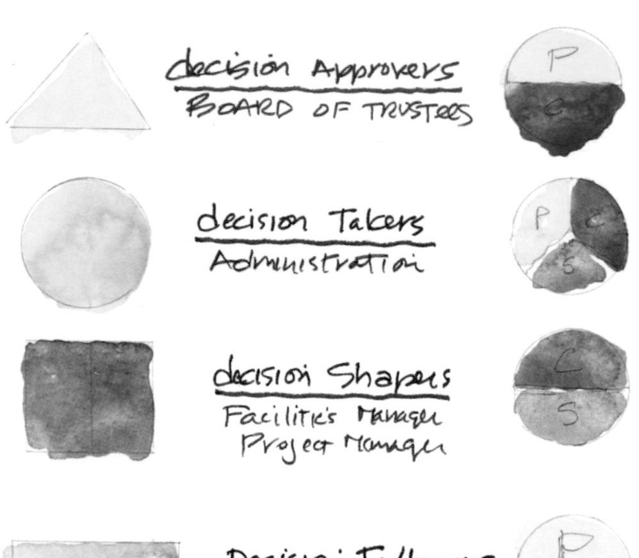

Sim Van der Ryn water color diagram of player in the design process.

design process works to show the potential for dysfunction when key information and agendas are not openly shared and discussed by all the players at the outset of a design process. The architects/planners take the easiest route through the bureaucratic political maze, avoiding obvious issues where conflict exists.

Take the case of the University of California's agenda to build a new campus in the Central Valley. Sustainability is a politically correct buzzword, so it was stated as an important performance goal for the project. But instead of choosing an available urban infill site, the planners chose to build miles from the nearest urban center on an ecologically fragile site. The result: a planning disaster that destroys valuable open space, feeds sprawl, increases and lengthens auto commutes, and displaces local, low income, rural farmworker housing. Now they say they are going to build green buildings!

The solution is that from the outset of a project, all the players gather with the help of skilled facilitators and graphic recorders in focussed workshops to get all ideas out in the open. It means busting through organizational lines of communication and envisioning many possibilities to arrive at shared goals, clear communication, and explicit shared agreements regarding process. Risky? Yes! Worthwhile? Ask the people who've done it. It's a new and important part of design and education: designing the design process.

This inclusive process—including visioning, master planning, and programming—is important in exposing not only areas of agreement but also areas of disagreement. With old-fashioned command and control planning, a few powerful people make the decisions, generally based on little key information, with minimum or no input from the users, and employing a host of inefficient or dysfunctional products. By not trying to sell a predetermined agenda and solution, the inclusive process simply tells the story about a particular project in a particular time and place. Do the ideas resonate? Is there a consensus and commitment to move ahead? Are there competing alternatives? The graphic record displays all the steps and concerns, honoring every voice in the process.

chapter 5

PLACES OF HEART AND SPIRIT

During the late 1970s and into the 1980s, a cultural and spiritual awakening had taken root in many places, and the West Coast was a primary incubator. I was fortunate to be of service to many groups in helping them design master plans and facilities that spoke to their beliefs and practices.

One reason I enjoyed this work was because I was interested in many of the practices and philosophies espoused by these groups. Another attraction was that many were located in unique natural landscapes. I don't dislike cities, but I have an affinity for working in areas where natural environment predominates. A poem I wrote in 1987 explains:

I like to build places
where nature is foreground
and cannot be overpowered
by our temporary creations.

I use geometry not only to
organize space and to mark
the social interactions within
but also to resonate with
the landscape.

The building is not a fixed
object but part of the larger
pattern that flows with change—
a permeable membrane
responding to changes in use and place.

I like to use natural materials
native to a place—earth, stone, trees
with advanced technology and scientific intelligence.

Architecture is part of the process of
"re-membering"—putting back together
our collective dreams.
I like to design buildings that are places
for learning, healing, reflection,
coming together.

The building should tell a story
about place and people
and be a pathway to understanding ourselves
within nature.

san francisco zen center

A Japanese Buddhist teacher, Shunryu Suzuki Roshi, established the San Francisco Zen Center in 1962. Before Suzuki Roshi's death in 1971, the center had purchased a monastic site in the Santa Lucia Mountains east of Big Sur. The place, Tassajara, had been inhabited by the indigenous people because of its hot springs. After European settlement, it became a fishing camp and resort with cabins, a bar, and a dining hall overlooking Tassajara Creek. Owned by Bob and Anna Beck, we discovered it in the early 1960s and loved its wildness. Then we heard that a Buddhist group had purchased it. I met Richard Baker, who was appointed by the beloved Suzuki Roshi before his death to be the new abbot. Dick Baker was a tall, energetic, engaging man with wide-ranging interests in literature, art, psychology, architecture, and, of course, Buddhism. We immediately liked each other.

Over the years, I designed many projects for Zen Center. Through Dick's leadership, Zen Center was growing rapidly and developing a strong economic base. While exclusively a monastery most of the year, in the summer months Tassajara was open to guests who were also free to participate in meditation sessions and lectures. The first project I did was a cluster of new cabins in the Japanese style. Baker's head builder, Paul Discoe, had studied temple carpentry in Japan and had assembled from their community a skilled set of builders. A unique feature of the courtyard cabins was compost toilets, which I had suggested because of the cluster's location close to the creek. They were the first application of my compost privy design.

Exterior of Green Gulch Guest House.

George Wheelwright, the cofounder of Polaroid, had given Zen Center a magnificent ranch that ran from a coastal ridge top to the ocean about fifteen minutes north of San Francisco. Here, at Green Gulch, Baker planned to establish a monastic center close to the city and an organic farm to supply his growing community. There were only two buildings, the ranch house and a large barn. Part of the barn was converted into a *zendo*, or meditation hall. The rest of it was divided into small students' rooms. I was asked to design an addition to the ranch house that would include guest rooms, a dining and kitchen facility, and a smaller meeting place for lectures. The new building, named in honor of George Wheelwright, was connected to the ranch house by raised covered walkways. Again, we used Japanese forms and simple shapes.

The most striking building project I designed at Green Gulch is the guest house with twelve guest rooms and a central meeting space. The building is an octagon, a centering form that is easier to build out of wood than a circle.

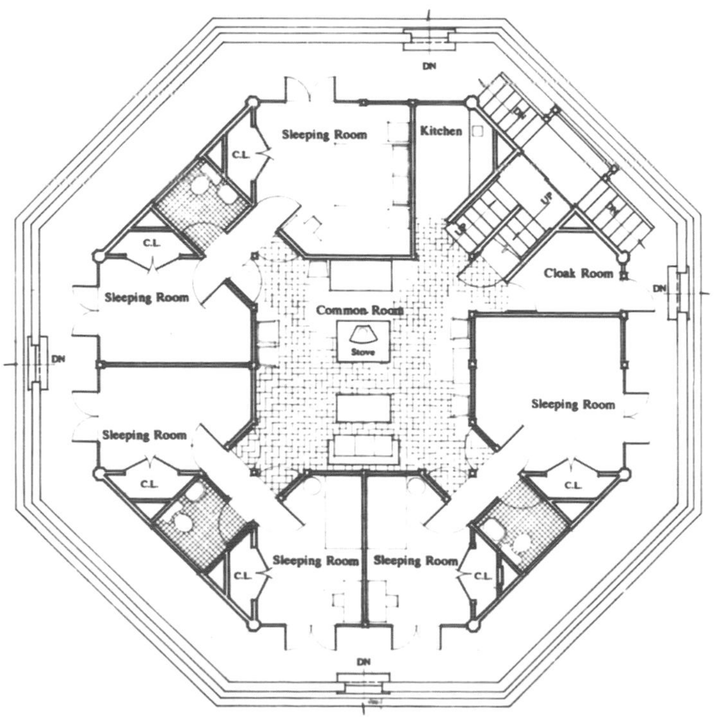

FACING
Walkway,
Wheelwright Center.

ABOVE
Green Gulch Guest House,
interior.

LEFT
Green Gulch Guest House,
floor plan.

In 1979, Zen Center established Greens, one of the nation's first gourmet vegetarian restaurants, in a historic military warehouse at Fort Mason on San Francisco Bay. The plan is a simple rectangle with an existing wall of windows offering views of the Golden Gate. The most arresting feature is an informal seating and table area fabricated by my Inverness neighbor, J. B. Blunk, out of old redwood burls left by loggers. The rich organic forms and textures are a perfect foil to the simple geometry and materials of the restaurant and also resonate with the movement of the restless waters in San Francisco Bay directly in front of the diners.

RIGHT
Green Gulch, Abbot's House,

FACING
Greens Restaurant, San Francisco, California. Photograph © Jon Naar 1979, 1999.

As in all the Zen Center projects, the design and construction resulted from a unique collaboration between Baker Roshi, Paul Discoe, and myself. In the old Japanese tradition, the master carpenter designs from a repertoire of well-established dimensional rules, formal patterns, and elaborate joinery techniques. When we started working together, Paul Discoe commented that I was the only architect he had ever, or would ever, consider working with. I only had to produce hand-drawn scaled plans, elevations, and sections. Paul did the rest, translating my drawings into framing plans and details. Using largely reclaimed lumber, he painstakingly prefabricated the frames in his shop. He and his crew made all the doors, windows, and cabinets.

This design/building process brought out the best in each of us. Baker, as the client, knew what he wanted and clearly communicated it. I asked him at the outset if Zen Center intended to get building permits. As state architect, I'd been outed for not getting permits for my own buildings. He looked at me quietly and said, "Buddhists build to last a thousand years. We don't need permission to build."

Because the rooms are guest rooms for people who are not primarily Zen students, my initial thought was that there needed to be acoustical separation between spaces. Baker disagreed, opting for the traditional Japanese mode of light shoji screens providing visual but not acoustical separation. "The lack of acoustic privacy will teach mindfulness."

He prevailed, as did his prediction. The story goes that during one guest retreat, a couple arrived late at night after everyone was asleep. They engaged in lengthy, arduous, noisy lovemaking, waking up the other guests. When the moans signified mutual climax and completion, the other guests spontaneously applauded and cheered.

Looking back on the Zen Center experience after twenty-odd years of practice, I realize that the old master builder model gets the best results with the least friction and waste. There are too many players in today's projects, too many conflicting concern. Prompted by fear of litigation, each participant generates reams of unnecessary paper and compartmentalizes responsibility in needless ways rather than working towards a common vision.

lindisfarne center, crestone, colorado

The Lindisfarne Association was a unique group of explorers laying the foundations for a new culture that preserves the ancient wisdom of cultures being destroyed by modernism. Founded by the cultural historian William Irwin Thompson and supported by Laurance Rockefeller, the annual one-week meeting of this unique group was my intellectual support group. It provided a rich diet of dialogue, new ideas, and inspiration that I chewed on for sustenance all year long. The Lindisfarne Fellows included a small pantheon of my heroes, mentors, and friends such as Gregory Bateson and Mary Catherine Bateson, Gary Snyder, Wendell Berry, John and Nancy Todd, Wes Jackson, David Orr, Stewart Brand, Paolo Soleri, Richard Baker, Michael Murphy, Stuart Kaufman, and Mayumi Oda, among others.

In the early 1980s, Bill Thompson was given land and funding to build a center near Crestone in the Sangre de Cristo foothills of southern Colorado. He asked me to design the center's main building, incorporating a home for his family, a space accommodating forty to fifty people for the annual Fellow's meeting, a large kitchen, a greenhouse, and a garden. Crestone is a remote place with extremely cold winters and winds that sweep across the San Luis Valley. The cold winter is ameliorated by lots of sunshine.

BELOW and FACING
Lindisfarne Center, Crestone, Colorado.

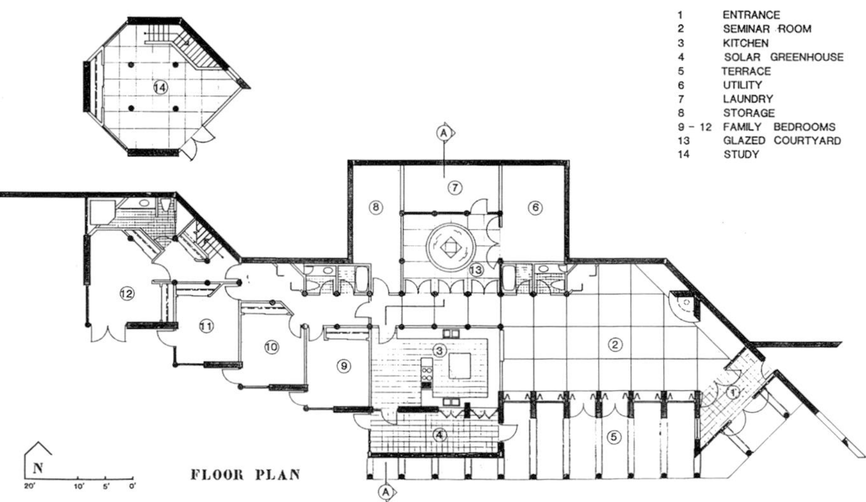

At the time, Crestone was waking from its long sleep as a ghost town and there was little skilled labor in the area. However, we met Michael Ogden, a transplanted Californian and experienced contractor. The finished Lindisfarne building is rough hewn, and with stone walls the same color as the peaks above, the earth-sheltered building virtually disappears into its site.

The site and climate suggested a basic passive solar building with a long east-west axis to maximize direct winter sun. The north wall of the building is not exposed to the bitter winter winds, and it and the roof are covered with soil. We planted native buffalo grass on the roof. We used two local building materials: native rock that tumbles down from the higher elevations and was abundant at the site, and pine killed by beetles from Kit Carson National forest for the major beams or *vigas*.

Some years after the building was complete, Bill Thompson and I had a wide-ranging conversation (published in *Annals of Earth* 7, no. 3, 1989) about my work, touching on how I design and work with clients, the building process, and then-popular ideologies such as feng shui and deep ecology.

Here are some excerpts:

Sim Van der Ryn: When you innovate, it doesn't matter what goes wrong—real or imagined, the innovation takes the heat . . . the [Lindisfarne Center] project was a milestone in creating buildings in truly unique environments, sites that are themselves places of retreat, reflection, and learning.

Bill Thompson: It was an improvisational process of working with local people, using regional materials, and encountering the spontaneity of nature in which you can't play the Renaissance role of a Palladio to achieve total mathematical perfection. We went to the top of the mountain to use the local beetle kill trees with our local tree man . . . he responded to our specifications for the maximum log by incorrectly measuring the tapered top of the trees rather than the much larger base. Our critics think the beams are massively out of proportion. What we did achieve is a sense of place often lacking in America.

SV: In designing, rather than slavishly replicating sacred formulas, I improvise according to what the people, the place, and the process have to say. I work like a jazz musician who does not play every note the way it is written, but improvises on a theme.

BT: When the New Age shifted from exploration to doctrine, we ran into the old problem that "A little knowledge is a dangerous thing." We as architect and client had agreed on the positioning of the house. We were being sensitive to deeper geomantic natural flows. When the construction manager insisted on shifting the house six feet over to save one small tree, one of the bedrooms got positioned not merely over a water course, but over a water spiral, a strong vortex where the water really goes around in swirls and people wake up screaming in nightmares at four in the morning. His decision was a compassionate act, yet was insensitive to other kinds of natural flows. If you are going to sentimentalize your abstractions of nature, you are not going to see nature's raw creative power. Nature just doesn't seem to keep the books in terms of individual trees and animals.

SV: Exactly right. Like the problem with experiencing buildings as objects, people tend to also experience landscapes as static pictorial reality. Deep ecology seems to fall into the same sentimentalization of natural process.

dharma sangha, crestone, colorado

In 1997, Bill Thompson, for health and personal reasons, turned Lindisfarne over to his old friend Richard Baker, who had left the San Francisco Zen Center and established a center in Germany. Baker also continued to have students in the United States, so Lindisfarne seemed an ideal place to establish another monastery, which he named Dharma Sangha. While the original building had a meeting space, it was not big enough for large meditation retreats, so Baker came to me for help in designing a new zendo. The budget was limited. In a weekend at my home in Inverness, we sketched out a very simple form, with dimensions based on the golden mean. Richard found a local barn builder who erected the shell of the building. Then, Len Brackett, a builder and cabinetmaker experienced in Japanese joinery and carpentry, did the interior, including cedar-planed ceilings, raised meditation platforms, and other details. The overall result achieves serene simplicity through an economy of means.

ABOVE
Interior, Dharma Sangha, Crestone, Colorado. Photograph © David Hoptman, 1994.

findhorn foundation housing, findhorn, scotland

In the 1960s, a New Age community grew up in a trailer park in Scotland near a Royal Air Force base next to the nearby town of Findhorn. Led by Peter Caddy, a former RAF officer, and his wife, Eileen, Findhorn offered an experiential potpourri of different ideologies and teachings, and achieved notoriety for the size of its very large organically grown cabbages, which they claimed were nurtured by friendly spirits. Some local wags suggested the cabbages grew that large because of the broken septic tanks that provided their nutrients, but I was never able to verify that rumor.

Peter and Eileen had built an interesting meeting hall and wanted to build housing that reflected their values. I was invited, along with Jim Hubbell, to work with the Findhorn community to develop a complex for a cluster of new housing. Jim is a multitalented artisan in metal, glass, and stone—a sculptor, painter, poet, and building designer. He has spent a lifetime building a fantastic homestead of workshops, family quarters, gardens, ponds, and sculpture gardens in Julian, California, which lies in the mountains east of San Diego. (Sadly, only ruins remain after an October 2003 fire near San Diego swept though the Julian surroundings.)

Our design workshop began by using the method I had developed for group work as a way to break through the often wordy and rambling character of group conversation that is linear, with each person waiting for the other to finish. We created three walls, labeling each for one of three subjects: "Facts," "Goals," and "Concepts." Participants were given five-by-eight-inch cards and asked to write or diagram as many facts, goals, and concepts as they thought relevant to the project.

ABOVE AND RIGHT
James Hubbell's Findhorn model.

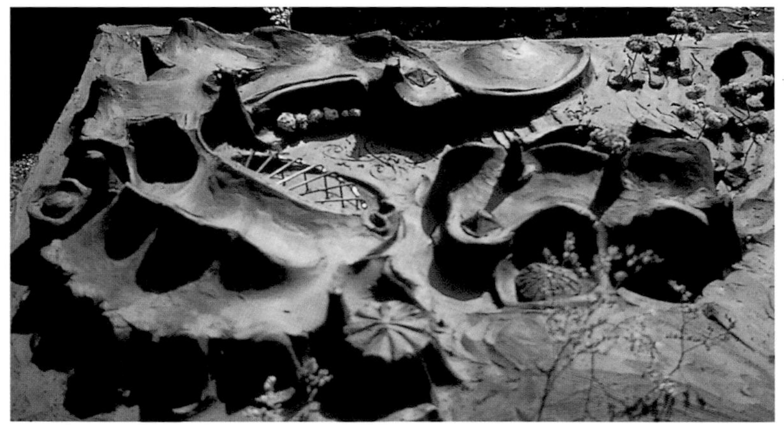

When they were finished, we grouped similar ideas into clusters of cards on the wall and then as a group began a discussion of each set. One interesting outcome was the difference between the community members who were interested in facts and those interested in goals. The fact people were the practical hands-on folks who, for example, knew where the frost line was. They were the people who kept the pace running. The goal people were much more conceptual and vague. There wasn't much communication between the two groups.

The workshop was a warm-up for Jim Hubbell and me to begin our work in developing the design for a new housing cluster. I focused on facts, such as the extremely low winter sun at Findhorn's far north location and space layout that included private and shared spaces. Jim started out with modeling clay, and using my rough plan layout, developed a flower-like structure that reached toward the sun. The preliminary plans were approved at a community meeting, and we returned home to work on the design.

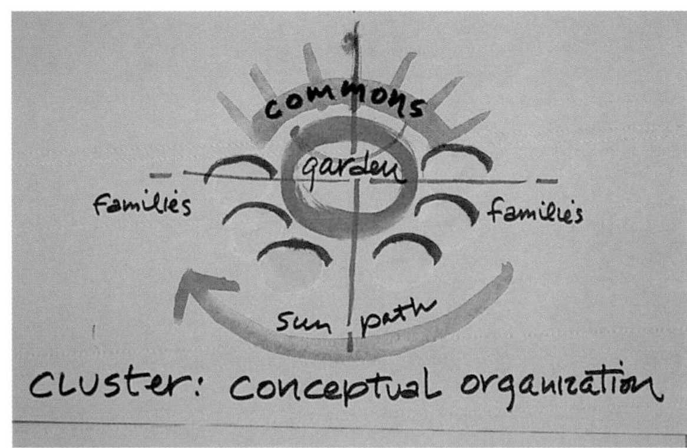

Sim Van der Ryn's Findhorn concept sketch.

Jim's designs are remarkable structures. Frameworks of reinforcing rod are woven into the overall shapes and then sprayed with concrete to create stable shapes. Then Jim and his apprentices gave the forms extraordinary color and life by using adobe, hand-forged metalwork, sculpture, stained glass, and shaped wood—all fabricated in Jim's workshops at his home. We did a more complete model and series of watercolors of the concept and returned to Scotland. It was beyond the imagination of even the most conceptual Findhorn people, and they ultimately rejected the design as too radical.

James Hubbell's Findhorn watercolors.

Ojai Foundation School model.

ojai foundation school, ojai, california

Ojai lies in the interior coastal hills in Southern California east of Santa Barbara. Long a home for spiritual and psychological studies, the Ojai Foundation School was a fairly informal group, living and learning on a long dragon's-back ridge near Ojai. Joan Halifax—anthropologist, author, and student of Buddhism—was the most visible leader in the group. She had been granted money by Laurance Rockefeller, a benefactor of many of the projects in this chapter, to develop a permanent center out of the collection of temporary structures, hidden in the trees along the ridge. Joan asked my design class to come to Ojai and conduct a design workshop with the community to draw out the community's ideas.

As we progressed during the day, it became apparent there was little consensus in the community about their goals or what concepts might implement them. Deep divisions arose among different groups in the community. Rather than try to engineer a predetermined agenda or controlled result, we were simply reflecting back the community's own conflicted state of being.

I didn't hear from Joan for another year. Then she called and said that as a result of the workshop and the disagreements it uncovered, there had been changes in composition and structure of the community. Now they were ready to begin design. A smaller group convened, and we developed a building program for the school that provided housing for students and faculty, a large meeting hall, dining room and kitchen, and office.

Some weeks later I returned to Ojai for another design workshop. Our first task was to find a site for the school. I suggested that everyone spend several hours in silence walking the land and when they felt they had found the place where their body and mind told them the center should be, to sit down. After several hours, the largest group was gathered in a gentle bowl between two ridges. Armed with maps of the area that included topography, I started sketching an arrangement with housing steeping gradually up the hill from an elliptical central form, which served as communal open space. On either side of the ellipse were public spaces.

Returning to the office, Pete Retondo, an accomplished builder, architect, artist, and former student, developed the plan in drawings and model. Architects like to say that you interview for ten projects in order to get one, and for every ten you get, you get to build one. Unfortunately, Ojai Foundation School did not get built as the community went through another upheaval and Joan Halifax left.

The Ojai project is my best unbuilt project, the first that bridges the gap between first and second generation ecological design. First generation focused rather mechanistically on maximizing separate aspects, or technologies, such as access to the sun. Second generation represents a much higher level of integration—a true shift from the idea of buildings as fixed mechanical objects to the idea as buildings as organisms that adapt and change through differing conditions and changes in the environment.

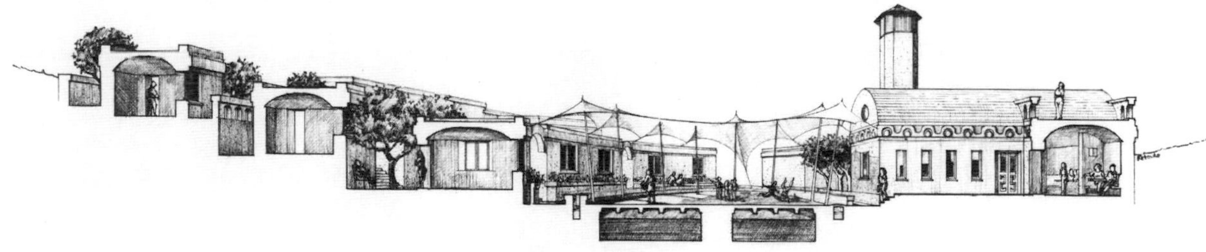

Ojai cross-section.

TOP Ojai systems sketches.
BOTTOM Floor plan.

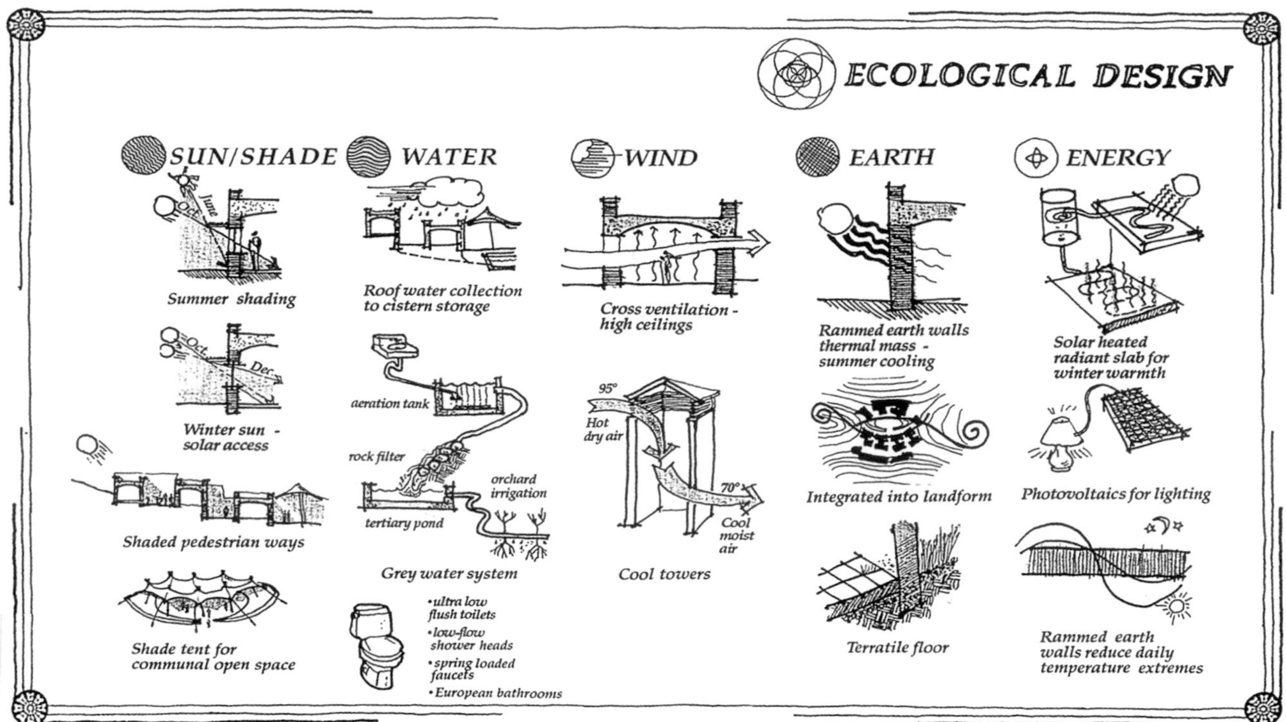

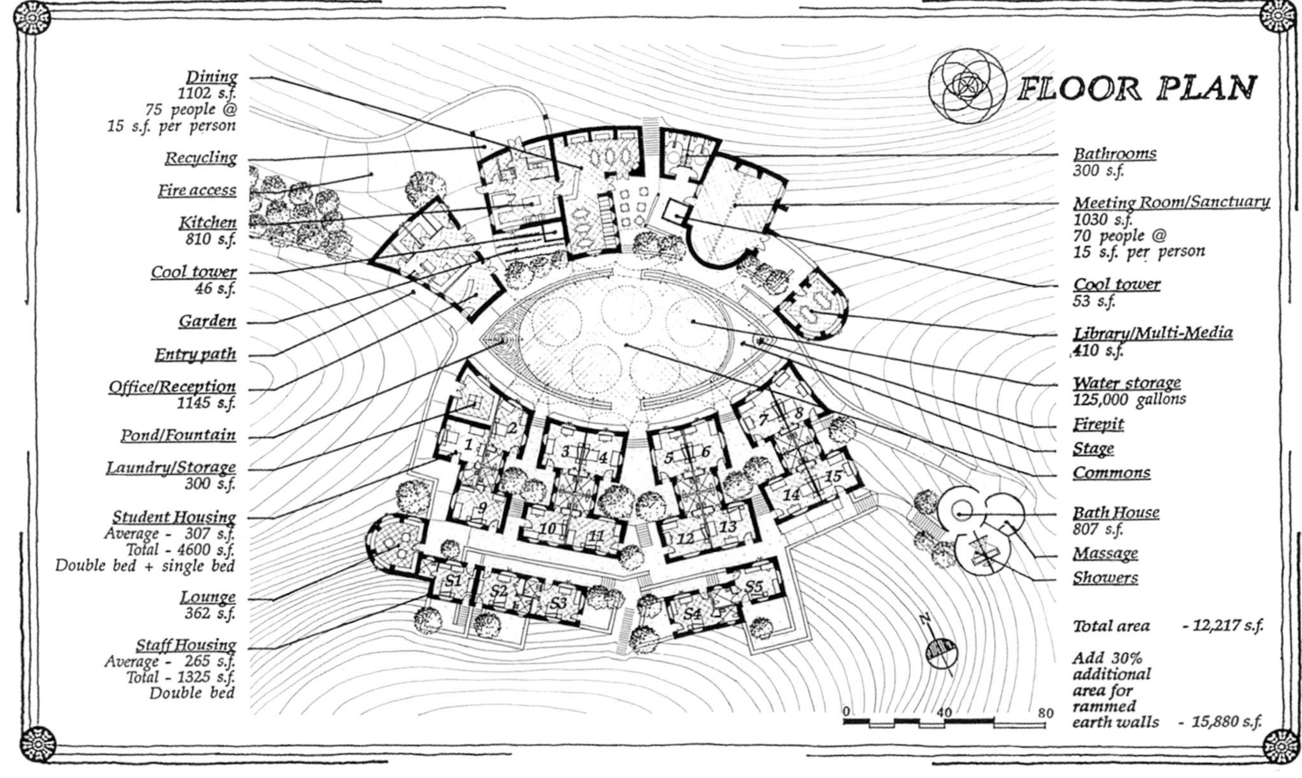

mind center, palo alto, california

Brain wave feedback is a process by which the rhythm and frequency of one's brain waves are recorded and fed back in audio form to the subject. The so-called alpha frequency is associated with a state of deep meditation. I participated in a ten-day Alpha Brain Wave Training with one of the pioneers in brain wave research, Dr. James Hardt, at his Agnew State Hospital laboratory. Although long associated with Zen Center as their architect, I had seldom joined in the daily meditation sessions, so the experience with Dr. Hardt was my first real immersion, and I was quite amazed at the results of spending ten days, eight hours a day, listening to my brain waves.

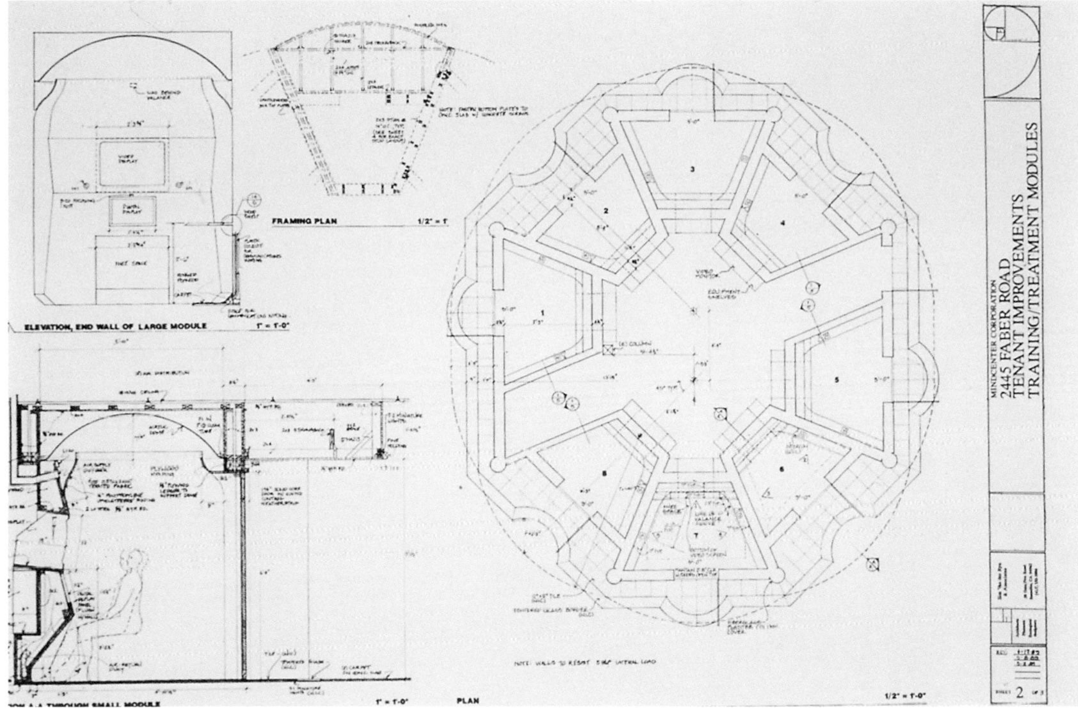

LEFT
Plan of Mind Center complex.

RIGHT
Interior of Mind Center module.

Foster Gamble, another student of Jim Hardt, planned to create a series of Brain Wave Centers and retained us to develop a prototype. The procedure requires the participant to sit long hours in a soundproof cubicle with a computer, listening to the amplified sound of his brain waves. There are break periods during which the participant answers questions on the computer screen. We designed the facilities to merge space and time with soft contours, special surfaces, and complex electronics. To ameliorate the claustrophobic feeling—which few people expressed awareness of once they were engaged in the practice—we created a horizon and a gradual sunrise-sunset effect to mark the end of feedback listening periods. The cubicles also had soft edges and carpeted walls and floors. The first prototype was built in a typical office space in Palo Alto. For me, it was a departure from most of my design assignments—working with a technology in an environment sealed off from nature. But we were not sealed off from our own brains and minds, which, after all, are very much part of nature.

life expression chiropractic center, sugarloaf, pennsylvania

ABOVE LEFT
Chiropractic Center exterior.

ABOVE RIGHT
Chiropractic Center interior.

FACING
Chiropractic Center green roof.

Ron and Joanne Gallagher are natives of Hazelton, Pennsylvania, and both were children of coal miners. Through their life experience, they have developed deep and abiding ecological values. Ron is a finish carpenter, and Joanne, trained as a nurse, found her life's work in chiropractic care. For over fifteen years their dream was to build their own chiropractic center that would demonstrate their life values. They went on a search for an architect that shared these abiding values. They knew of the Real Goods Solar Living Center and through them found Van der Ryn Architects.

I offered to visit their site, at which time we would work together on the site to develop a concept design. What a leap of faith it was for them to invite me over the phone, not knowing what to expect!

The site was a working farm near their home in a conservative rural community. It was a warm summer day. I asked Ron to put up a sheet of plywood on some sawhorses under a shade tree. We walked the site and I soon had an idea where the building should be. I asked them how they ran their busy practice. Waiting and reception areas were very important in setting the feeling for the space. I sketched two treatment wings facing south and then a third wing for an entry. Having been a patient, my feeling was that the entry space should flow with forms that felt in sympathy with the nature of the human body. I sketched a curved roof and suggested the idea that it be a living surface of native plants

The Gallaghers fell in love with the entry space and green roof as expressions of what the center was all about. We ended the weekend exhausted and elated. Flying home, I wondered how they would pull it off in their conservative community. Luckily my associate, Dave Deppen, is a native of central Pennsylvania and, like the Gallaghers, is a radical in conservative dress and manner. Dave worked hard with the Gallaghers to develop the design so that it could fit their modest budget and also the prejudices of conventional builders and the planning board. It took four years to bring the vision to reality. We found Charlie Miller, a green roof pioneer in Philadelphia, who created the living roof. Ron was on the construction site everyday. His keen eye and dedication to seeing the vision through resulted in a level of craftsmanship rarely seen in today's construction.

When patients go there today, they enjoy a unique, beautiful space. As one patient said, "This place feels so peaceful. Coming here is part of my healing."

ecological burial : memorial ecosystems.

RIGHT
Watercolor of cemetery.

BELOW TOP
Memorial Ecosystem logo.

BELOW BOTTOM
Remembrance.

The last project is one on which we are working now. I include it because I believe the concepts embedded in it are going to make a major impact in our culture—especially on how we presently relate to death. I was approached by Dr. Billy Campbell, of Westminster, South Carolina, who had brought to America a new idea about the environment of death. First, he believed that in dying we had the opportunity to give something back to nature through the endowment fees paid to the cemetery and also through our physical bodies returning our material substance to nourish the soil and what grows in it. He had taken an old cemetery in Westminster and, with his wife, Kimberly, painstakingly begun restoring native species on the site. Contrast this with the modern cemetery model, which is more like a golf course with nonnative grasses maintained with herbicides, pesticides, and regular mowing. The Campbells saw their cemetery as incorporating natural burials—without preserved bodies or nondegradable caskets—and placing them in restored native landscapes.

Word of their work spread through the death industry. A young cemetery owner in Los Angeles with Midwest roots was inspired by what he read of their work and purchased the original cemetery near where I live, a thirty-seven-acre parcel adjoining national park lands and overgrown with invasive trees and weeds. I invited the client team and my design team to a weekend in Inverness to set goals for the project.

A year later, our plan is in process. The three themes are ecological restoration of the site, making the cemetery a lively community place rather than a place one avoids, and then remembrance of our loved ones, not through conventional headstones but more personal and natural tributes. The main mortuary building, a 1960s modernist structure, will be transformed with water elements and a flowing wall of native mosses and ferns. The remarkable thing about this project and similar ones we hope to do is the degree of resonance that these ideas have had with people who are not in denial of their eventual death, and recognize that what these innovators propose is better for both heart and spirit.

The projects in this chapter go to the heart of the idea of architecture I believe in. First, in each case the process was a true collaboration among client, architect, and builder. This type of personal relationship and commitment is usually missing in larger institutional projects. Second, concern for maintaining the integrity of the natural place was foremost in everyone's thoughts. A third characteristic is that of building in the continuous present. We start with a concept and prepare drawings, but as building progresses and ideas flow, the design is open to change and improvement. In the usual institutionalized design process, that is practically impossible because the whole process is driven by fear: fear of cost overruns, fear of making mistakes that may lead to lawsuits, fear of innovation. All the examples in this chapter are more like a medieval building process, relying on master builders rather than a highly fragmented and specialized workforce. The process relies on shared goals and, above all, on trust among the parties. Without these elements, the results will embody neither heart nor spirit.

ecos

technos

mythos

spirit

design

nature

chapter 6

MAKING THE GREAT LEAP FORWARD

"The scale at which humankind is restructuring the planet gives us only two choices: become stewards of the earth or destroyers. To integrate human aspirations with natural systems we must model our work on the greatest designer of all — nature itself."

—Anthony Brown, director, ECOSA INSTITUTE, Prescott, Arizona

Much of this book so far is the history of my life in design. The stories relate how my questions led to action and to built experiments that were early seeds in the emergence of green architecture and the sustainability movement.

In this closing chapter, I address fundamental questions about where design has been in the past and where it might go in the future in relation to major changes taking place in our culture and in the world, to imagine what our next step might be. This chapter addresses four interconnected questions:

1. Can we make a great leap forward in our thought and our actions towards reversing the destruction of our Earth home and build a new civilization in the process?
2. What has been the role of design in the evolution of human societies since our species appeared on Earth?
3. What are some key concepts for integrating nature's processes with design?
4. What are the attributes of the next major advance in design called *Integral* or *Eco-Logic Design?*

hope and the evolutionary path

Hope: the feeling that what is wanted can be had or that events will turn out for the best. —*Random House Unabridged Dictionary*

Hope just means another world might be possible, not promised, not guaranteed. Hope calls for action; action is impossible without hope." —Rebecca Solnit, *Hope in the Dark*

Hope isn't the same thing as wishful thinking because it recognizes reality for what it is and proceeds in faith and creativity to better possibilities. —David Orr, *The Last Refuge*

My life in design has, from the beginning, been driven by questioning the implicit assumptions that propel design, and the hope of finding better answers to the ways we design and the products we produce. Nothing we design is ever finished. It just keeps evolving, just as everything else in life changes. The stories in this book relate my journey, fueled by hope, to teach and learn, design and experiment, and to create built form that points towards a more ecological world, physically and spiritually.

I'm often called a pioneer: "a person who first enters or settles a region." That region exists in the mind and heart. For many years I've searched for models that help frame a bigger picture than that of my immediate experience. I rejected formal religion as a child, and later the worship of Progress and an unquestioning faith in materialist mechanistic science and technology.

After Ronald Reagan's election to the presidency in 1980 and the Republican administration that replaced Jerry Brown as governor, much of what we had accomplished in Sacramento and after—the energy-efficient building program, the Office of Appropriate Technology, as well as the Marin Solar Village—unraveled. After years of success implementing my ideas and thought experiments, nothing seemed to be working. I felt despair and hopelessness. Aimlessly, one day I leafed through the dictionary looking for "hope," and found the definition quoted above. What struck me was that in the definition, "hope" had no timetable or ego attached to it. My work had always been propelled by self-imposed timetables. Ego was attached to my definition of hope, as was linear time.

Many in my generation, who came of age in the 1960s and 1970s, experienced a rainbow of hope. Young, energetic, and possessed with common visions, we thought we could change the world and ourselves. In many ways the world changed and so did we. But the spirit and energy of those times unraveled with assassinations, violence, and a worldwide bonfire of the vanities that left some of us angry and depressed, while others jumped on the boom bandwagon. Cultural historian William Irwin Thompson writes, "True cultural transformation is deeper than shifting lifestyles and consumer trends, and deeper than changes in a ruling class or the invention of new technologies."

Through my disillusionment I searched for a historical and philosophical framework that could sustain my hope for our planet and its human inhabitants, one that would give purpose and direction to my work. I was in territory that is familiar to many of us: What is there to believe in outside the narrow boundaries of the self and our present dominant culture? The modern existential dilemma defines our existence: we are as half god and half worm.

My search put me in contact with a now largely ignored school of philosophy, the Perennial Philosophy (Arthur Oncken Lovejoy, *The Great Chain of Being;* Arthur M. Young, *The Geometry of Meaning;* Jean Gebser, *The Ever-Present Origin;* Pierre Teilhard de Chardin, *The Phenomenon of Man),* which envisions a progression in human evolution that transcends the view that evolution is simply an elaborate game of chance in which the lucky genes keep reproducing (Richard Dawkins, *The Selfish Gene),* or an endgame that follows the rules of Darwinian selection.

The view expressed by the German philosopher/historian Jean Gebser in *The Ever-Present Origin* is that while humans haven't changed biologically, humanity has gone through huge nonbiological mutations creating radically new cultural structures and worldviews. At the dawn of history there is no separation between humans and nature. The sequential development of symbolic language, agriculture, war, science, individualism, capitalism, technology, and cities increasingly disconnect human communities and nature's communities, disconnect body, mind, and spirit. He predicts a new consciousness reintegrating culture and nature, human spirit, body, and mind. The material and the transcendent worlds reconnect in our being. This new stage he called Integral Consciousness.

In Integral Awareness we experience both the impermanence of the material world and our interconnectedness to it and the flow of the universe. The perennial philosophy aligns with other ancient spiritual traditions such as Buddhism, Hinduism, Kabbalah, and Gnosticism. In recent years, chaos theory and fractal geometry provide additional support for the view that the world that the rational mind assumes is fixed and knowable and separate from us is not.

I have faith in the possibility of human culture and consciousness transcending a long obsession with objects, quantities, and control, moving towards an ecological intelligence and

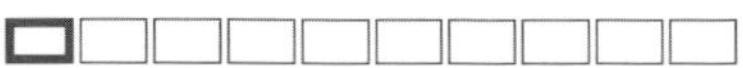

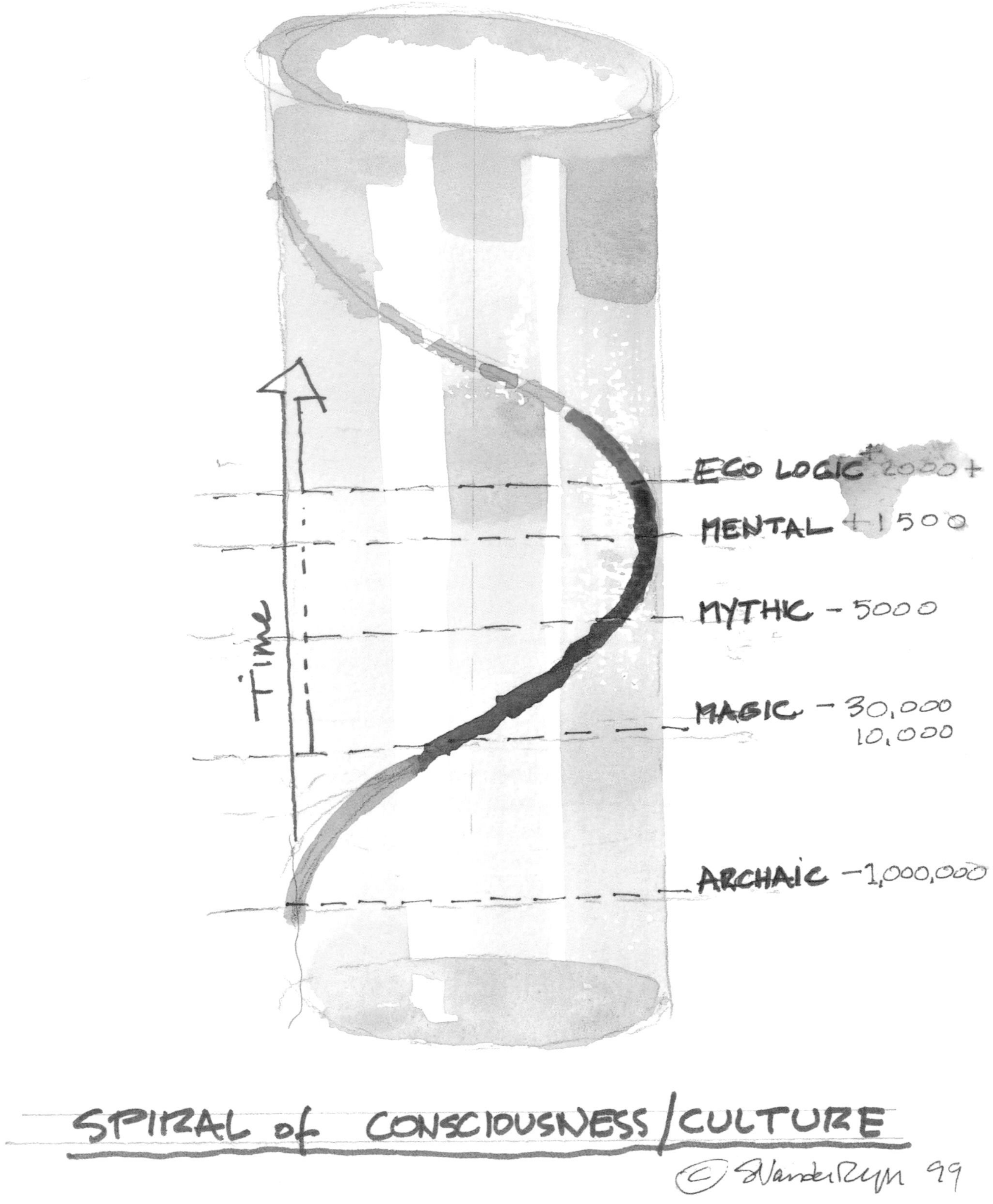

Time

ECO LOGIC+ 2000+

MENTAL +1500

MYTHIC -5000

MAGIC -30,000
10,000

ARCHAIC -1,000,000

SPIRAL of CONSCIOUSNESS/CULTURE

© SVanderRyn 99

compassion for everything that is alive and changing, including each of us. The heart of ecological design is not efficiency or sustainability. It is the embodiment of animating spirit, the soul of the living world as embodied in each of us waiting to be reborn and expressed in what we design.

We have gained much so far in our journey as a species, but we also sense the shadows, the losses, and the inner hollowness that comes with the hubris of believing we have control and power over people and all other forms of life. The growing evidence of damage to basic planetary life support systems brings into question popular views of how human culture and nature are connected.

We are waiting to be re-enchanted—to join our higher selves, our souls, to the evolving living world. My hope is that another profound process of cultural mutation can bring each human being to live and act on that essential truth and bring about an Ecological Age in which both our species and the living planet thrive and continue to evolve.

Spiral of Cultural Evolution

The diagram visualizes the Perennial Philosophy as a cylinder of four-dimensional space. Humankind is like a spiraling gene through time and space. Each turn represents a new epoch, a nonbiological mutation of consciousness superimposed on the existing forms. In the most developed form, all previous forms are transparent and accessible. Everything is experienced as a self-similar (fractal) aspect of the whole.

where on earth are we?

Technology and the global economy are rapidly changing the condition of human life support, human culture, and what it means to be human. The sights and trends are not pretty. Satellite images reveal the blotchy, rapidly growing, gray patches of megacities—sprawling, polluted prototypes of an increasingly urban future. The same building templates are replicated globally, regardless of place or culture. Good farmland and soils continue to be depleted at accelerating rates. Grasslands turn into deserts, forests into wastelands, rivers and coastal waters into stinking cesspools. Species are disappearing at a rate unparalleled since the catastrophic collision of meteors with Earth ended the age of the dinosaurs millions of years ago. And everywhere on earth, complex human communities and natural ecology are destroyed and processed into economic commodities.

Ecologic Footprint (EF), developed by Mathis Wackernagel and his colleagues, has become a standard metric to assess the relative sustainability of any place or economy. In its simplest form, it measures the amount of different types of land required to

- Produce energy and absorb carbon dioxide from fossil fuels
- Provide space and support for the built environment
- Provide food, fiber, and forest products
- Provide fresh water and purify wastewater

It measures the load imposed on natural systems by a given population, a given level of consumption that closely correlates with income, and a given level of design and technology. A change in any of the factors alters the total footprint. Population (P) in developing nations—which have high consumption rates—is leveling off, and even decreasing in some instances. The poorest countries with small footprints typically have the most rapidly growing population. The design (D) factor is critical. Housing whose electricity comes from the solar panels, energy-efficient cars, community plans that reduce automobile use, foods produced with low inputs of fossil fuels, programs that reward recycling and manufacturing for disassembly and reuse, all can greatly reduce footprint.

Data developed by Wackernagel shows that it takes 6 to 10 hectares of different categories of productive land (15 to 25 acres) to support one individual living a Western lifestyle. If we take the global population of over six billion people and allocate all lands on the planet, 1.7 hectares of land per capita is available. If we assume that everyone on Earth wants to live like us, it would take 3.5 Earths to meet basic demands. Today, perhaps a half billion people—one out of every six—leave a big footprint. The other five and a half billion make do with far less. The United States, with 4 percent of the planet's population, uses 40 percent of its resources. Only through a redesign of everything can we avoid catastrophe. China, with 25 percent of the people on the planet, is rapidly modernizing and has a huge appetite for oil, steel, water, wood, and all the resources needed to support a modern technological society. India, with eight hundred million people, also is developing rapidly. We are already in a era of wars over resources: oil, water, forests, fisheries, to name just a few. Climate change caused by global warming is here to stay with deadly effects for many places. It's time for an ecologic leap forward and the Integral Era that will coevolve with it.

We glimpse the possibilities of an ecological world, but as yet it has no global form, physically or as community. The ecological world is within us, waiting to find form and opportunity for expression. Once uncovered, it will emerge in its own way, creating its own time and its own forms.

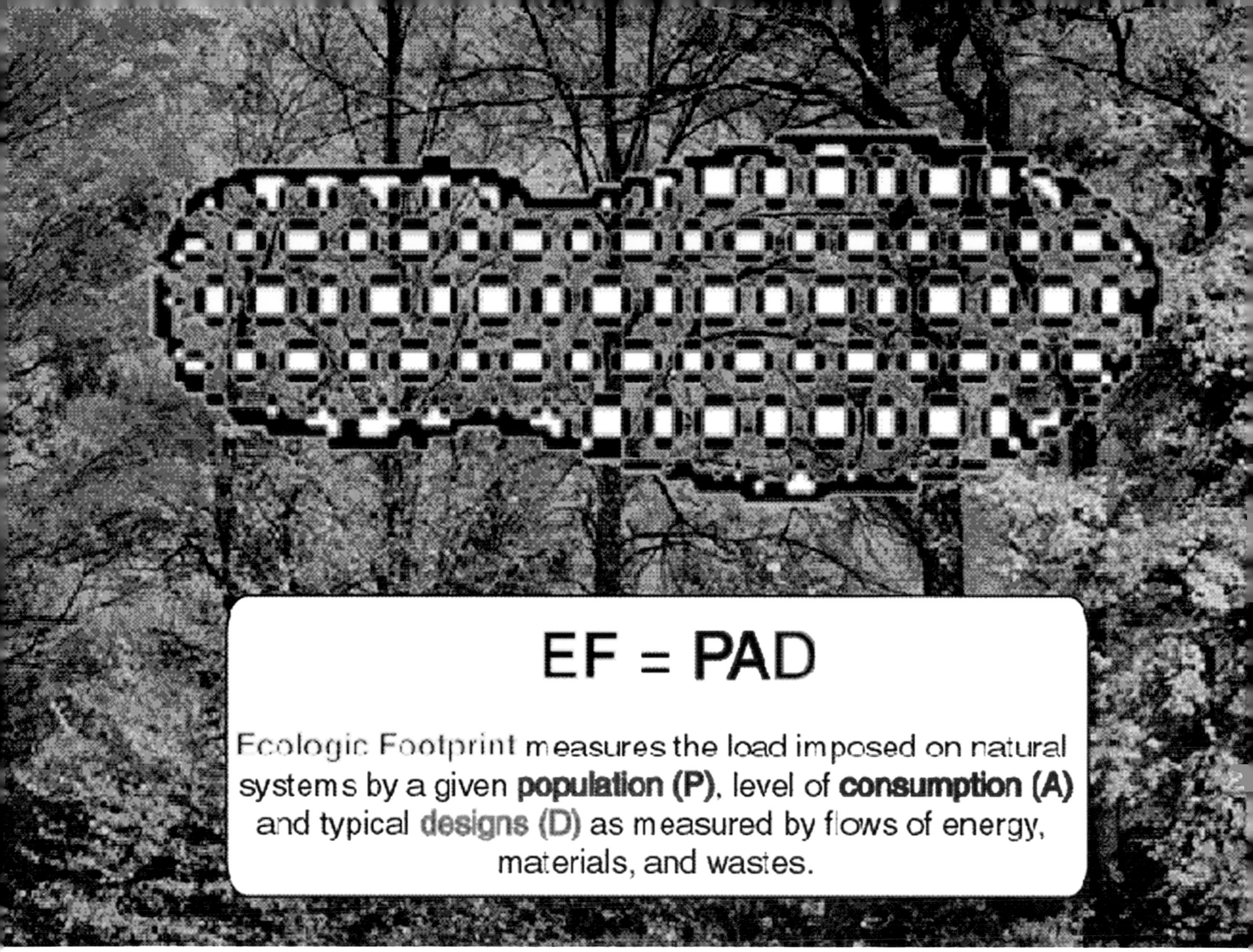

EF = PAD

Ecologic Footprint measures the load imposed on natural systems by a given **population (P)**, level of **consumption (A)** and typical **designs (D)** as measured by flows of energy, materials, and wastes.

Our Ecologic Footprint

The world's ecological footprint (WEF) can be expressed as an equation: WEF=PxAxD, where P is Population, A is our level of Affluence, and D is our level of Design and Technology. Consumption correlates with income. Generally, the wealthier you are, the more you consume. Efficient and eco-effective design solutions and technologies can vastly reduce consumption. Reducing population is the other factor; however, poorer, lower-footprint countries tend to have growing populations, while the most developed wealthy nations have lower birthrates.

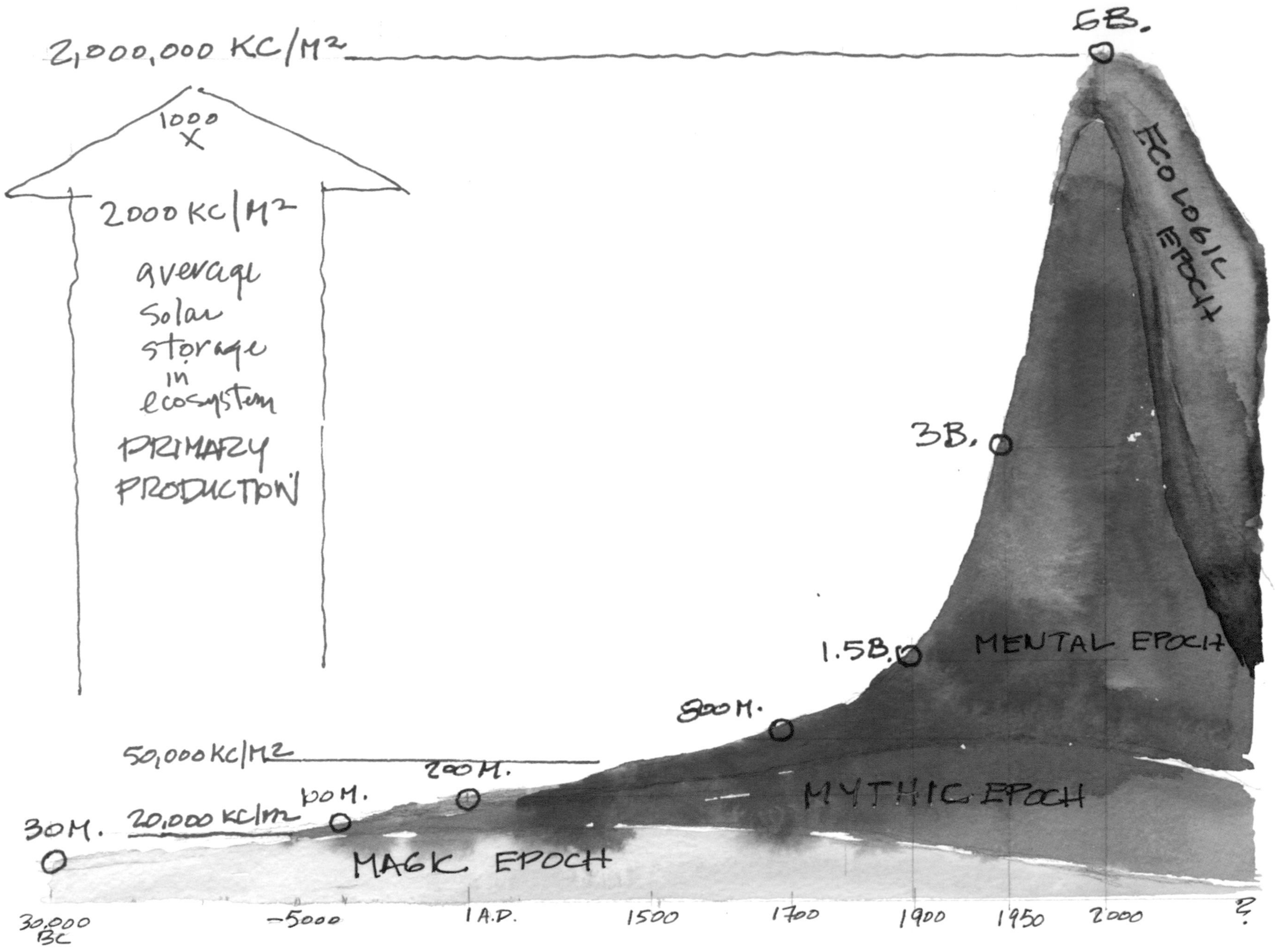

The Ecological Leap.
The graph maps the following variables:

- Estimated world population over time
- Ecologic footprint at selected points of history
- The emergence and decline of the three major epochs in human history: the *Magical*, *Mythical*, and *Mental*.

The horizontal axis of time is not to scale, but the vertical axis of consumption is to scale.

"A gent l'e cuma li patati I derbis gli och quand gli e int an dela merda fin pasa al col." —Valtellina dialect

"People are like potatoes. Their eyes really open only when they are up to their necks in shit." —Northern Italian folk saying

As the wise folk saying suggests, when we can no longer deny the mess we're in, our eyes really open! Before discussing how ecological design in an integral age can lift us out of the manure pit, let me summarize graphically where we are. It will open your eyes.

The metric for Ecologic Footprint I use are calories (KC) consumed per capita per day. Our earliest ancestors consumed 2,000 KC per day, all of it food to support the rate at which they burned energy (metabolism) and replenished cells. Coincidentally, 2,000 KC is also the amount of solar energy stored per day in a square meter of plant biomass, not of all which is food. By contrast, in today's modern civilization, it takes about 2,000,000 KC per day to support a person's way of life, only a thousandth of which are the food calories. This number correlates with the 10 hectares/per person of productive lands required to support a single human in modern society.

The horizontal time scale compresses most of our human history. The vertical scale does not. So what we see is a slow growth in global population and steady consumption throughout the era when the hunter-gatherer Magical era was dominant. Population and consumption spiked a bit with the invention of agriculture and resource investment in tools, building, and implements of war. In 1700, as the Industrial Revolution was building steam in Europe, world population was 800 million and per capita consumption jumped to 70,000 to 100,000 KC per capita per day. This was due to the use of coal, building the infrastructure for new industry, the extensive navies, and urban growth of the new powers.

By 1900, the population has doubled to 1.5 billion, and consumption continued its exponential rise. It took only fifty years for the population to double again to 3 billion in 1950 while consumption kept up with the mass distribution of automobiles, road systems, suburbs, and a growing industrial/military complex. Another fifty years brings us to the present, with another doubling of population and another exponential rise in our Ecologic Footprint. Today less than a month of world population growth equates with the total world population in 30,000 BC, when we had already inhabited the planet for more than a million years.

The graph shows a sharp inflection point some time in the next generations. David Brower used to talk about "making an ecological U-turn," in the sense that we would begin to use our limited resources more wisely, and use less of them. The peak of the graph is followed by a downward U in which population and consumption both fall. The path of steeply rising consumption and population simply cannot continue. It's not just a question of improved technology and design; it is a question of a worldwide shift in values, a time when most people really do open their eyes to what is happening to our Earth home and actively choose and create another path. A new epoch, the Integral (or Ecologic) Age will take root.

the three rings: design is the mediator between culture and nature

Years ago I developed a simple three-ring diagram to help students understand that their role as designers is as mediators between what the culture and clients tell them they want and what nature tells us it needs.

As with any design context, it includes three basic elements or questions: Why? What? and How?

Why? refers to the reasons we do something. It is at the center of the three rings and initiates any action or design. Exploring the Why? for a culture means looking deeper into the underlying reasons that societies do what they do, based on shared perceptions of how things are, what they believe to be true about the world and how it works, and what is valued and important and what is not. A shared worldview stands for the basic agreements that underlie a culture and its vision of itself. It is the inner ring that initiates action.

What? refers to the physical material context of design: the constraints of site and environment, the natural environment, and the interconnected processes and products available to meet a need. Every design problem has specific physical constraints, all are embedded in the particular con-figuration of physical systems. These include climate, soils, topography, geology, hydrology, and vegetation. Nature presents the larger physical reality, its opportunities, and constraints. It is the outer ring that supplies and supports culture.

How? is the mediator between Why? and What? Design and technology mediate between a culture's needs and the physical context and content that provides the materials and ingredients for a design solution. The How? is design and designing: the technology, art, tools, and processes to materially satisfy human needs and wants.

A diagram of the three elements provides a guide to use in the study of the relationships between design, culture, and nature for a given historical period or for a particular design situation. The three rings provide a simple analytic and descriptive tool to relate the design of a civilization to its environment and underlying beliefs.

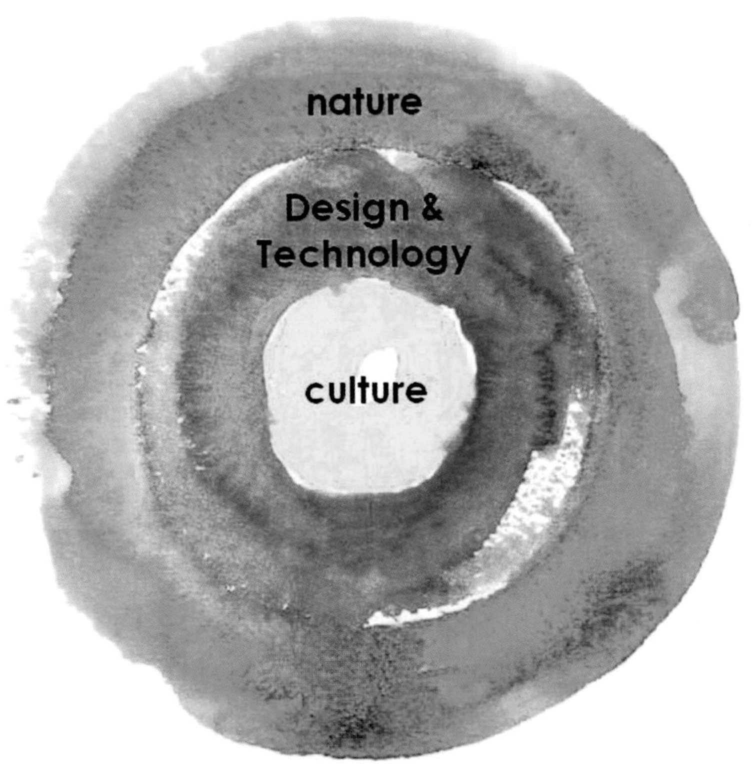

Three-Ring Diagram
Design is essentially a hopeful activity. Much of our time as designers is spent imagining and planning future states of physical being, which we assume will be better than what we have now. We live on the edge between idea and materiality in a state of hopeful dreaming and play. We are the interface and intermediary between human spirit, living nature, and built form.

the four stages of human history

Since our emergence as a species a million years ago, humans have evolved through four distinct forms of consciousness: Archaic, Magical, Mythical, and Mental. A fifth stage, Integral or Ecological, is emerging. In each shift, the older consciousness structure is still within us, although the latest form dominates. The earlier forms of consciousness are repressed, leaking out in deficient or negative ways.

The hard wiring of humans has not really changed since our emergence as a species. Each stage in the development of human consciousness is associated with archetypal cultural and built environmental forms, which coevolve together. In this mutually coevolving process, consciousness shapes the environment humans create. In turn, environment shapes consciousness. At each stage of consciousness (Archaic, Magical, Mythical, Mental), cultures design and build archetypal environments. Looking at the past, present, and future of design as process and product provides insights into where we have been and where we may be going. Later in this chapter we will look at a possible Integral future, but now we take a quick tour of where we have been.

history's epochs viewed through eight lenses

We look at each stage of human and cultural development through eight lenses that describe its worldview and culture, its design characteristics, its ecology, and economy.

The turning point is the event that triggers the next stage in human development. The difference between our species and our closest relatives was the development of a larger brain—a biological mutation. The turning point triggering all other epochs are nonbiological mutations. Gebser writes, "In contrast to biological mutations, these consciousness mutations do not assume or require the disappearance of previous properties or potentialities." In other words, each new cultural form is layered over the last form, but not in a transparent way.

An analogy is our individual human development from conception to birth, and then through the stages of life, a process the nineteenth-century biologist Ernst Haeckel called, "ontogeny recapitulates phylogeny." In this process, the development of an individual organism appears to mimic the evolutionary history of a larger group of organisms. From conception to birth, we individuate from a single cell into embryos that seem to recapitulate the historical development of all life from lizards, to birds, to mammals, and then finally humans. Then, from birth and in our early years, we move through the Magic stage of childhood into the Mythic stage of adolescence, and then into the adult Mental Rational stage. Future generations may move into the Integral stage, where the earlier forms they passed through are still accessible and transparent to them. Today, only the most gifted artists, visionaries, and spiritual masters live in that transparent world.

- The lens of **Cultural Form** refers to the prototypical social/institutional structure of any particular stage.

- The lens of **Space and Time** is crucial to how we view the world. For example, a key factor in the emergence of modern consciousness was the development of perspective: space and time viewed as fixed dimensional realities from the viewpoint of an observer at a fixed point in space and time.

- The lens of **Morphology** describes the significance of the built forms typical to each stage.

- The lens of **Geometry** observes the prototypical geometric forms favored by each stage.

- The lens of **Built Form** illuminates the typical type of individual or community form built in that stage.

- The lens of **Design Process** illustrates the characteristics of the typical design process used.

- The lens of **Ecological Footprint** notes a society's metabolism or consumption.

- The lens of **Economics** describes the system of exchange of valued goods or services in any stage.

Ecologic footprint measures per capita consumption in each stage. The metrics used are average per person daily use of energy expressed in KC. The modern world's ecological footprint is also described in terms of the total land area per capita required to provide energy or absorb carbon dioxide resulting from fossil fuel use; land consumed by the built environment; land required to provide food, fiber, and basic raw materials such as timber.

archaic consciousness

Archaic	
Leap Forward	Larger Brain
Culture Form	Band
Space / Time Concept	
Design Morphology	
Prototype Geometry	◯
Prototype Built Form	Natural Shelter
Design Process	Instinctive
Ecological Footprint	2,000 - 10,000 KCal / Cap / Day
Economics:	

The transformational factor that begins human history and the era of Archaic consciousness several million years ago is the emergence of a larger brain, which separates us from our primate cousins. Without a symbolic form of verbal or graphic communication, our species stayed in the Archaic state for most of our history. The cultural form was the roving foraging band. Archaic Consciousness lives in a world without space or time. They didn't build but sought natural shelter such as caves. Design process, if any, was instinctive. The daily per capita Ecological Footprint was 2,000 to 5,000 KC per day from gathered foods and fire. The three-ring diagram for the Archaic is an all-encompassing ring of nature because there is no distinct culture or technology beyond instinct for our earliest human ancestors.

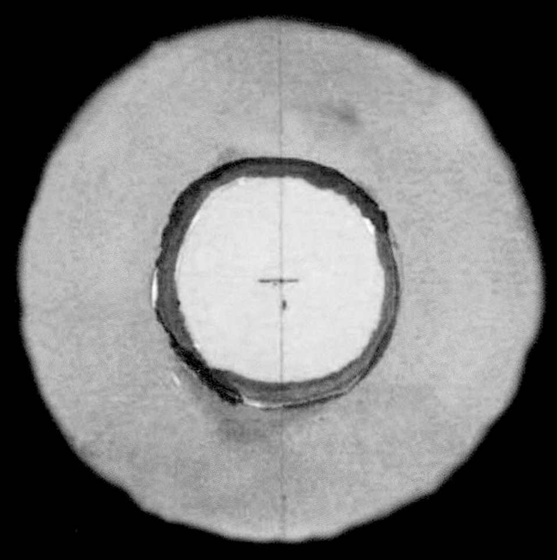

The World of Magical Consciousness.

magical consciousness

Magical	
Leap Forward	Symbolization
Culture Form	Tribe
Space / Time Concept	Cycles and Centers
Design Morphology	Bio-morphic
Prototype Geometry	◯
Prototype Built Form	Village, Dwelling
Design Process	Intuitive
Ecological Footprint	5,000 - 20,000 KCal / Cap / Day
Economics:	Trade and Barter

Somewhere between thirty thousand and a hundred thousand years ago, humans experienced a major transformation: the ability to use sound or image to represent some object in their world—human, animal, or other. The transformational breakthrough of symbol-making creates the world of Magical consciousness. The heart of Magical consciousness is oral language and the graphic image. Magic makes no distinction between the symbol and what the symbol represents. This period initiates the beginning of conscious community: the hunter-gatherer tribe, and later the agricultural village. Space and time are defined by cycles and centers, but there are no linear boundaries.

Magical morphology is biomorphic since only natural materials were available, and forms were largely derived from nature. The archetypal geometry of Magical consciousness is the circle or spiral. The prototypical built form is the village of round huts that stand in a circle. The architecture of the hut, the yurt, the village, and its sacred monuments and symbols tend to be circular or spiral. This period saw the beginning of conscious design in the building of shelter and villages, often with symbolic references to nature. A good example is the African Dogon house in which each part of the house corresponds to a human organ. In another example, in Samoa the same word is used to describe placenta, house, and land.

In Magical consciousness the design process is intuitive. People create and build their own environments through a tightly interwoven fabric of long-standing cultural patterns, local skills, and available resources and technology. The process is "intuitive" because the skills and learning required to replicate a built environment are learned through everyday practice and experience in the culture, becoming part of one's nature. In traditional cultures, building was part of everyday learning and survival, handed down from generation to generation. Notice in the diagram that the middle ring develops like a thin membrane of information about the environment and simple tools to support the hunter-gatherer society that is typical of the period of Magical consciousness. Knowledge of the environment was often deep. The tribes that inhabited Patagonia had a language with over thirty thousand words, twice the modern vocabulary. Native shaman and healers knew the healing properties of thousands of plants, perhaps more than scientists collectively know today.

The major place that intuitive design lives today is in children's play. Remember building a sandcastle on the beach? Or piling up wood blocks into houses, or building a tree house? These forms of play are all ways of replicating environment, of re-creating and learning the meaning and substance of "house" or "home," learning our place in it and the process of its creation. I look upon design as a kind of informed play.

The ecological footprint of the Magical era was 2,000 to 10,000 KC per day for food, fire, and shelter. The three-ring diagram shows a cultural center of shared beliefs and practices. Nature looms large, with only a thin permeable membrane of material technology and experientially transmitted knowledge of the world separating Magical culture from its natural environment. Economics existed as barter and exchange between tribes. Ownership of goods was usually a community affair.

mythical consciousness

Mythical	
Leap Forward	Agriculture
Culture Form	Divine Dominator Empire
Space / Time Concept	Cycles, Calendars / Sacred Places
Design Morphology	Meta-morphic
Prototype Geometry	△
Prototype Built Form	Sacred Monuments
Design Process	Intuitive & Cosmological Formulae
Ecological Footprint	25,000 - 50,000 KCal / Cap / Day
Economics:	Trade

The next turning point occurred when humans learned to cultivate wild seeds, and later domesticate animals and grow crops. The invention of agriculture and the ability to store food surpluses leads to Mythical consciousness, starting in the Neolithic period and evolving into the great agricultural empires that developed five thousand years ago in the Tigris-Euphrates Valley of Mesopotamia, in China, in Central America, and elsewhere.

Stories became codified into myths, which provided meaning and identity to the groups that formed complex societies. With agriculture came the beginnings of mathematics and other sciences connected with observing the seasons and predicting planting and harvest times. Concepts of time were based on natural cycles. Lacking perspective, art was two dimensional (such as the Egyptian and Sumerian bas-reliefs). Space is defined by sacred centers and natural features.

Societies became organized into hierarchical layers with workers at the bottom, a layer of clerks and traders, a layer of priests to teach the societal myths and soldiers to enforce them, and at the top the king, emperor, pharaoh with all-knowing power derived from a mystical divine natural force. Some scholars, such as Rianne Eisler and Sally Goerner, also link the emergence of hierarchical agriculture empires with the development of war and dominator cultures. People's identities were completely linked to their class role.

The ability to grow and store food surpluses made agriculture the mother of architecture. The prototypical geometry of the Mythical agricultural empire is the pyramid, or layered tower, which we find throughout the world. The Mythical period produced the first architecture as we know it in the form of monuments and sacred cities reflecting their cosmology. I call the form concept "metamorphic"; the form derives not from nature as before, but from a transcendent mythology or cosmology. The process and its rules are carried out by craftsmen and master builders, probably without any written rulebook, but rather carried in their memory and experience. The great cathedrals of the Middle Ages are good examples.

Ecological footprint climbed towards 25,000 KC per day as the bandwidth of technology widened with the invention of technological implements for agriculture, war, ritual, cities, food systems, animal transport, roads, and monumental sacred complexes. All are connected to nature in Mythical cultures through belief systems such as the preeminence of Earth, or the fertility goddess found in many Mythical cultures. Economics included accumulation in the powerful institutions of religion and the state. We see the slow rise of merchants, each specializing in particular goods.

mental/rational consciousness

In Renaissance Europe, a new form came into being: the era of Mental/Rational consciousness. In the agricultural empire, there were no individuals in the modern sense. People were simply members of a given class with no separate identity. The Renaissance saw the rise of free

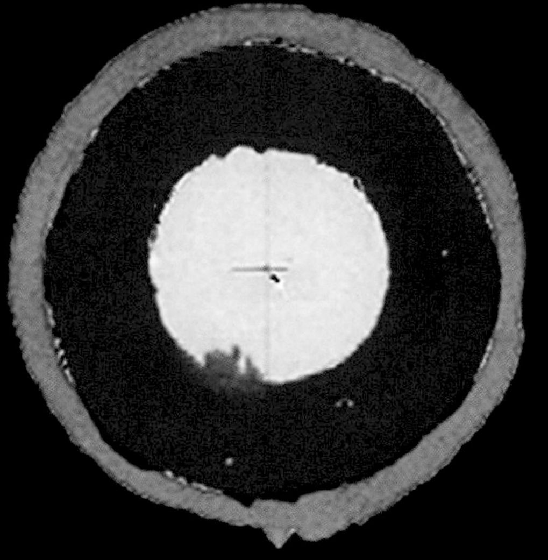

The world of
Mental/Rational
Consciousness

Rational / Mental	
Leap Forward	Individualism and the world above the given world of Nature
Culture Form	Secular State / Corporate System
Space / Time Concept	Linear / Measurable Space Time
Design Morphology	Mecha-morphic
Prototype Geometry	□
Prototype Built Form	Cube, Grid
Design Process	Metric, linear, piece-meal
Ecological Footprint	100,000 KCal / Cap / Day (early industrial) 2M KCal / Cap / Day (modern USA)
Economics:	Global money-funnel

and mentally enlightened individuals who make their own decisions, the development of city states, and later the establishment of corporations. This was the age of dualism in which body and mind are separate, the development of written language and printing, which separates phenomena and the written word. Descartes, one of the key philosophers of the period called the Enlightenment, declared, "I think, therefore I am." Painters invented perspective: the ability on a two-dimensional surface to create the illusion of three dimensions. This created a view of space and time as linear and measurable. Perspective implies the eyes of a single person seeing from a fixed position, a representation of the isolated individual, a new form of human being. Clocks were invented to measure time in discrete intervals. Science, with its "objective" descriptions of the phenomenological world, expanded rapidly. Space and time developed linear measurable dimensions where earlier spatial concepts focused on mythic centers rather than discrete boundaries.

With the Industrial Revolution, based on the notion of replacing human power with machines fueled by coal and oil, the Mental epoch picked up speed rapidly—first in Europe and North America, and by the end of the Second World War, spreading into Asia and most parts of the world. Its instruments included democracy (in which each person has an equal vote), corporate capitalism, and continued material progress through the systemic application of the scientific method to break knowledge of the world into smaller and smaller pieces of a larger machine. Nature was treated as a limitless resource to be exploited through the application of technology, capital, and labor to create new technologies, designs, and material objects that insulate us further from nature and take us farther down the road toward isolated individualism.

What is the prototypical geometry of the Mental era? Coinciding with the creation of spatial boundaries, this stage brings us the infinitely extendable rectilinear grid, with no center, no relationship to the land that lies beneath it, easily measurable. Thomas Jefferson was a surveyor and an architect. One of his first acts as president of the United States was to order a survey of the entire country, dividing it into square-mile sections. If you fly over the United States, you can still see the Jeffersonian land survey, where each square-mile is equal to every other square mile.

Its three-dimensional equivalent in built form is the cube or rectangular lattice, which has become the form for the modern buildings and cities. The city itself is a distributed, mechanically assembled, three-dimensional grid of mechanical parts and systems. The built forms of Mental consciousness are all around us: highway mazes, skyscrapers, the rectilinear grid that is suburbia, tract homes, shopping malls, and parking lots. With the intrinsic tunnel vision of hierarchical Mental consciousness, the products and processes of Mental design often become "dumb design"—more and more isolated from nature.

I describe the morphology of Mental design as mechamorphic—form follows from the mechanical process of production. The clockwork precision of the machine of parts is the ideal.

In *Mechanization Takes Command*, architectural historian Sigfried Gideon notes that mechanization and standardization are not only applied to building machines and buildings, they are also applied to the disassembly of organic nature as well as to the assembly of a clockwork mechanical universe outside of nature. Examples include Pillsbury's invention of the flour mill, which could separate the seed germ from the pulp to make white flour that would not become rancid. Also, the invention of the overhead disassembly line for the mass killing of pigs and cattle, which, according to Gideon, gave the young Henry Ford the idea for the overhead assembly line to produce the first mass-manufactured automobile—the Model T Ford.

Today's rational Mental design process follows the structure of mechanistic production:

- The whole is built of standardized parts
- Specialists design parts according to the rules of their discipline
- The process is sequential, integration of parts is linear
- The design replicates a standard template for a given building program
- The building is designed separately from its supporting infrastructure—energy, water, waste, food, transportation, community
- The finished product is a largely standardized commodity

A small percentage of architecture is designed by heroic celebrity designers ("Starchitects") whose mission is to create architecture as art that reflects their individualistic expression or signature. Their product is usually designed as three-dimensional static sculpture in which function and cost are sacrificed to heroic artistic vision. The inclusion of art as a separate unintegrated category of design results in building styles that reflect fixed, unchanging symbolic ideas. In the Rational Mental world, beauty no longer has any meaning. It is subjective and can mean whatever you like. As one well-known art dealer told me, "The meaning of art is that it has no meaning." This is a tragedy for the arts and architecture when the word *beauty* became taboo.

Americans, one out of twenty-five dwellers of earth, require ten to twenty times the productive land to support their way of life than residents of poorer countries.

Economics in the Mental Era is driven by wealth accumulation, which becomes the basis for class and power. As humans became more adept at controlling the environment, the nature of the economic system changed to one emphasizing accumulation rather than the flow of resources. In nature, there is no accumulation, only flow. The disruption of cycles of exchange of energy and materials in natural systems (in order to turn flows into accumulations of commodities that can be converted into money) is the root cause of our environmental crisis. The economic system does not levy a cost on the disruption of life. The accumulation of money becomes an increasingly abstract activity disconnected from ecological reality. As economist Jeffrey Steen has pointed out, more money changes hands in one day in speculative money markets than changes hands for goods and services in one year.

In the three-ring Mental diagram, the bandwidth of technology grows exponentially, increasingly obscuring and transforming natural processes and the configuration of living landscapes. The central band almost wipes out nature as a part of our consciousness. Today, in the late stage of Mental consciousness, the diagram is no longer static. Technology has triggered major changes in natural processes that, in turn, affect human technology and design. In earlier times, nature was seen as an uncontrollable force to be honored and respected as the source of all life. Now, in the era of Mental consciousness, it is seen as simply a collection of separate and unrelated resources to be used to improve the human economic and material condition. Now in the late stages of the Mental Era we are beginning to see a fragmentation of culture. The unconditional belief in human progress through technology and capitalism is giving way to a diversity of worldviews.

designing with, and learning from, nature

merging nature and design

Before discussing the emerging Integral epoch, I want to introduce a few key concepts that are critical to advancing design into its next stage. My last book, *Ecological Design,* coauthored with Stuart Cowan, articulated a new framework for design that is related to place, nature, and people. In this section, I introduce some more specific ways towards implementing design with nature.

The diagram explains the essence of what ecological design is all about: merging nature and technology. The left circle represents the Ecosphere, all the life-supporting services that natural systems provide humans. Most of these services cannot be replaced by any technology at any price. Ecostructure is humanity's endowment of natural capital, a gift of four billion years of evolution. If we use it up, or destroy nature's ability to keep providing us with essential services, we steal irreplaceable capital from future generations.

The circle on the right is Infrastructure or technosphere, all the designed systems created to meet human needs for food, shelter, mobility, communication, education, health, industry,

Natural Capital & Ecosystem Services
"Life support for the planet."

Air Quality
Water Quality
Photosynthesis - Oxygen, Food, Fiber Production and Energy Storage
Climate Balance
Biodiversity
Absorb and Process Toxins and Wastes

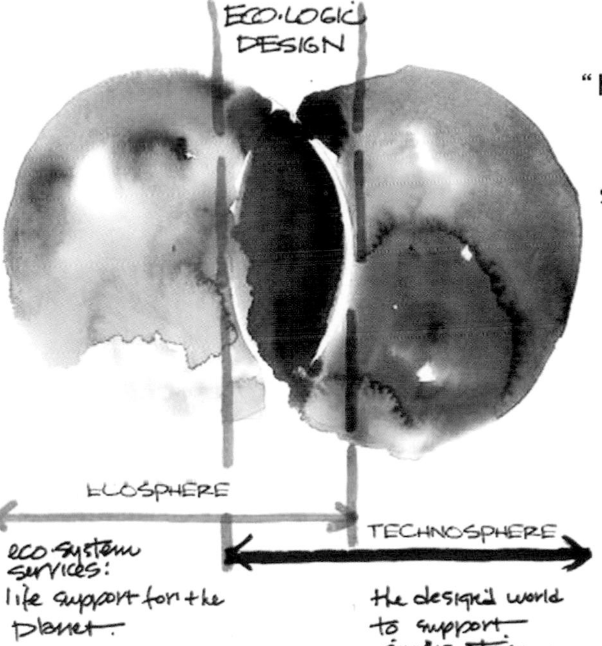

Design Capital
"Knowledge-based design and technology supporting human civilization."

Buildings- Design and Construction
Electrical Grid
Production and Distribution
Water and Sewer Systems
Transportation
Communications and Information Technology

security, and so on. Buildings and the infrastructure to support them (including energy generation and distribution systems, water, waste, roads, transportation, and communication systems) are a large part of the total technosphere circle.

The overlap between the two systems defines the sphere of ecological design: meeting human needs while maximizing the continuing capacity of natural systems to provide us their essential services. The areas of overlap defining ecological design include almost every area of human activity. Sustainable agricultural practices eliminate manufactured fertilizers, herbicides and pesticides, and extensive machine cultivation. Biological waste treatment uses wetlands to oxidize and absorb the excess nutrients in wastewater rather than large, engineered, chemically based systems. Natural burial cemeteries use our deaths to restore land to its original state. Green buildings work with natural energy flows, recyclable materials, and natural landscapes. Photovoltaic panels turn the random stream of electrons flowing from the sun into electricity. Zoos can become zones for ecological restoration rather than cages for animals.

The more we can get the two circles to overlap so that the functions of one enhance the functions of the other, the greater the potential of achieving the goals of a sustainable society by maintaining natural capital and inventing green technology and design to support life.

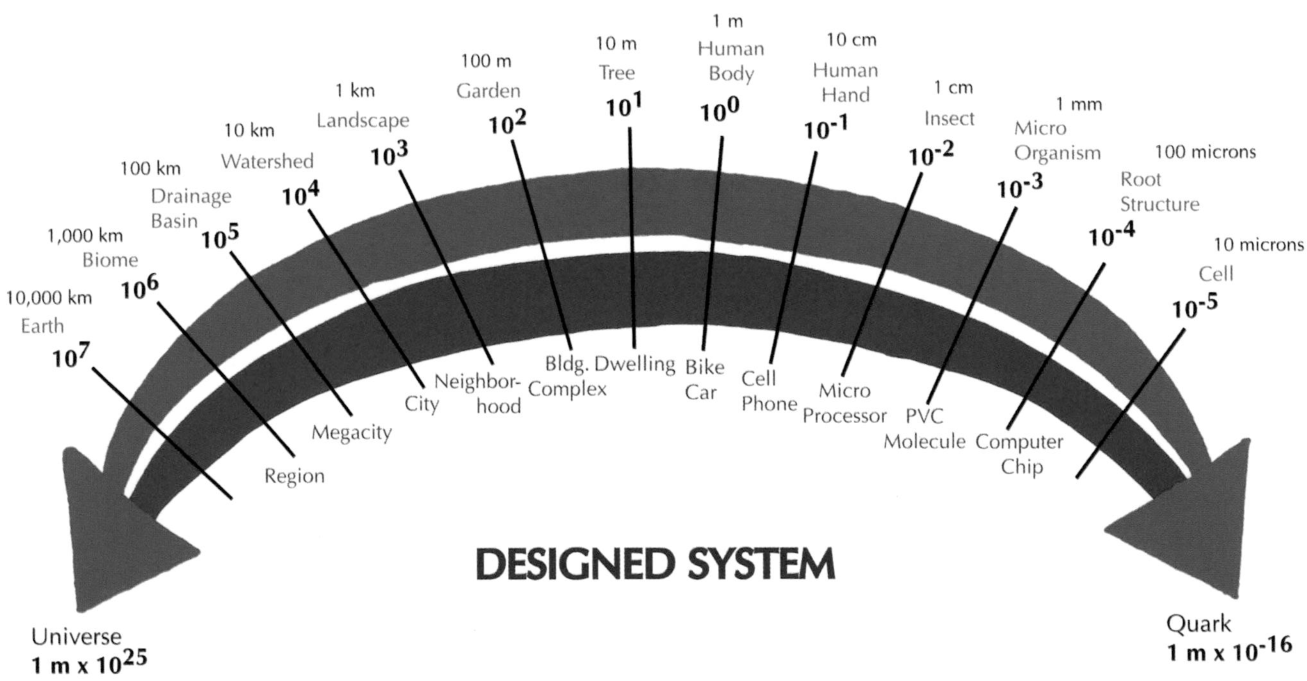

Continuum of Scales in Nature and Design

continuum of scales in nature and design

Both natural and designed places are defined by their physical scales. The designers Charles and Ray Eames, in a compelling ten-minute film and subsequent book, *The Powers of Ten,* compress the wonders of the known physical universe into forty-two exponential steps in scale from the infinitely large cosmos to the infinitely small quark. Any point on the scale is nested within the next larger scale, and the next smaller scale is nested within it, creating endless opportunities for understanding and exploring place. The idea of scale—of what is appropriate at different scales, and the relationships of scales to each other—is at the heart of design.

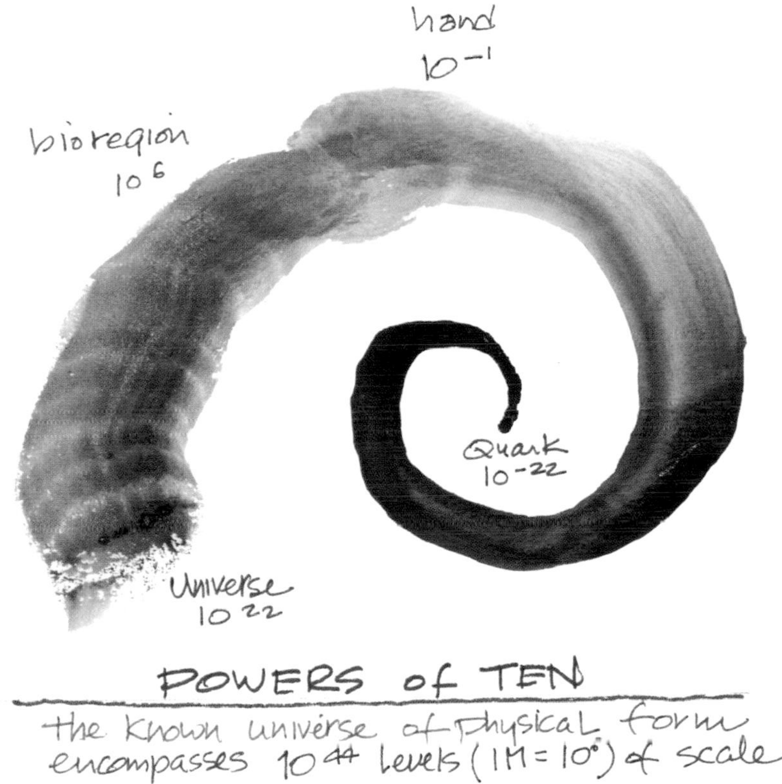

The diagram links Powers of Ten scales for both the designed and living worlds using common examples across a range of scales. The idea is to get us thinking about linkage across scales between the natural and the designed worlds. The character of truly workable places is that there is a fitness and integration between the built and the natural places at each level and at linked levels of scale. Powers of ten applied in this way allows us to see and think about our everyday world in a new way that unites our fragmented vision of reality. The study of place allows us to make connections between levels of scale and to enter into the process of making connections with the other two attributes: pattern and process.

bio-mimicry: learning from nature's patterns

"Nature as model. Bio-mimicry is a new science that studies nature's models and then imitates or takes inspiration from these designs and processes to solve human problems, e.g. a solar cell inspired by a leaf.

"Nature as measure. Bio-mimicry uses an ecological standard to judge the 'rightness' of our innovations. After 3.8 billion years of evolution, nature has learned: What works. What is appropriate. What lasts.

"Nature as mentor. Bio-mimicry is a new way of viewing and valuing nature. It introduces an era based not on what we can extract from the natural world, but on what we can learn from it."

—Janine Benyus. *Biomimicry: Innovation Inspired by Nature.*

"Discovery is seeing what others haven't seen before." —Jay Harman

Jay Harman ambles over to the whiteboard in his living room. The mantel behind the board is lined with objects that look like large whirling seashells and flower-like forms with leaves like propeller blades. He draws two Xs on the board and connects them with a straight line. He smiles. "Now most people think the shortest distance between two points is a straight line. And if you're on land that might be true, but it's not the case if you're moving through air or water."

Jay, an Australian, has spent his life in and on the water observing how marine organisms propel themselves through water. Fluids such as water and air move in spiral patterns. The spiral is of a particular type, a logarithmic spiral. In two dimensions, it describes the so-called Golden Mean, a harmonious proportional relationship used by the Greeks and other cultures in their architecture. In three dimensions, the logarithmic spiral becomes a vortex. Jay's observation of marine forms and wave motion led him to invent new designs for propellers and pumps using the three-dimensional logarithmic forms found in nature that move air or water in a vortex wave pattern with the least friction. His beautiful designs for propellers and pumps employ logarithmic forms that suck air and water through them rather than push fluids as do conventional pumps and propellers. They move far larger quantities of air or water with less energy than conventional designs, providing an inspiring illustration of how designers are learning from nature. As Jay observes, "Nature sucks, and it doesn't do it in a straight line!"

Sphere / explosion
Dynamic balance

Spiral / helix
Growth / movement

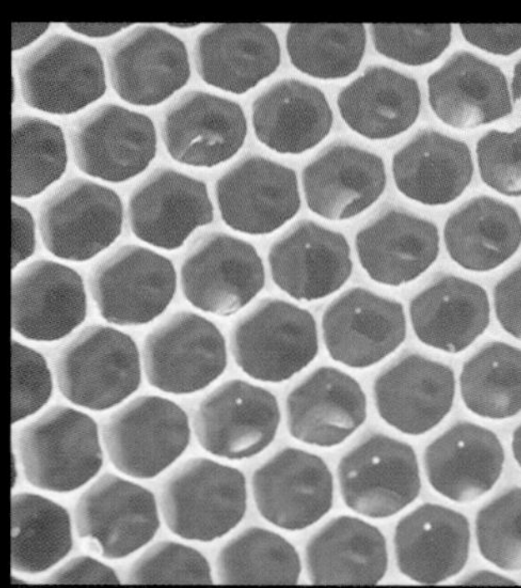
Net / mosaic
Regular division of area

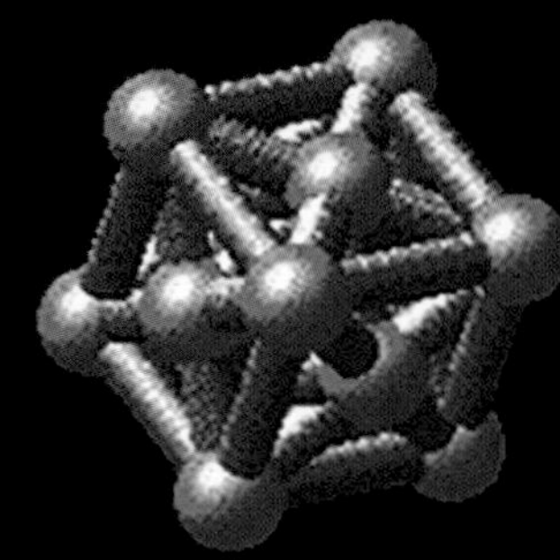
Lattice framework
Orthogonal division of space

Polyhedra
Spherical division of space

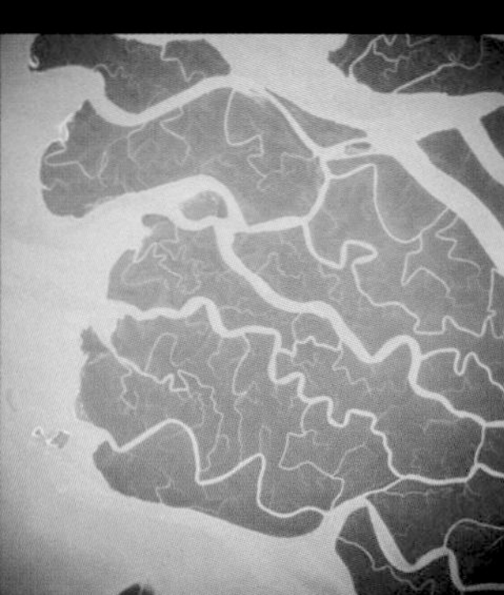
Meander
Flow

Branching
Circulation & Distribution

Wave
Cyclical movement

Symmetry
Self-similar parts

Fractal
Self-similar wholes

patterns of life

The next time you fly across the country on a clear day, let your eyes wander over the natural patterns and geometry of landscape and sky. You see the lazy winding meander of a river flowing through flatlands, sparkling wave motions on lakes and ocean, the branching patterns of a river delta, the complex fractal patterns of clouds and mountain folds. You see the human geometry of farmland divided into square-mile sections, the circular forms of pivot irrigation plots, the intricate branching of watersheds draining into rivers, the endless grid of streets from subdivisions to arterial roads to interstate ribbons of major highways.

It may look like there are infinite patterns in nature and the human-built environment, but that is not the case. From the smallest organisms to the scale of the universe itself, there are a relatively small number of basic patterns, each of which has a particular function. The meandering river expresses flow. Branching patterns in rivers and trees, like the branching design of our body's circulatory system, express efficient circulation and distribution. The grids of our farmland and cities express the regular partitioning of two-dimensional space. Helixes and spirals, from the organization of DNA to the spiral of a shell or the form of the galaxy itself, all express the dynamic organization of growth.

Studying the architecture of the living world in terms of what it teaches us about how to design our world has been my lifelong interest. It continues to inspire and inform my work. I'm not talking about making buildings or cities that imitate natural forms. I'm talking about a deeper process where geometry at all scales of the built environment integrates with the scale and processes of the living world.

Patterns of Life
Recognizing visual patterns at different scales is a key to seeing how things connect, and how and why they function. Seeing pattern in two, three, and four dimensions is a key to understanding systems. While the living world contains millions of individual patterns, most of them fall into one or more of ten archetypal categories. Each typical pattern tends to be associated with a specific function.

buildings and natural systems

"In a good building, as in nature, there is also living structure . . . Once we have that understanding, we may have a basis for thinking about architectural process and for identifying processes which are capable of creating a living world in the realm of architecture."

—Christopher Alexander, *The Nature of Order: Book Two*

We start with a little-known interesting fact. Regardless of size, every mammal lives for about 1.5 x 109 heartbeats. However, a shrew's heartbeat rate, or pulse, is many times that of a horse or a whale. Per unit of weight, it uses up many times more energy than larger mammals. That is, it has a higher metabolism. We use pulse as a synonym for metabolism, the physical and chemical flows and cycles within an organism that maintain life. All materials, systems, and cultures are engaged in complex temporal and spatial pulses. This suggests several principles that apply in designing buildings and communities that are meant to fit their environment. First, think of them as human-designed ecological systems. Second, diagram and, if possible, measure their metabolism—the input, conversion, and output of energy and materials. Third, optimize their ecological footprint—the impacts and interactions of their metabolism on other systems.

The key strategy in the ecologic design of buildings is to consider the building as an analogue of a natural system. Ecologists study such systems by tracing all the energy and material input and output flows through the organism or system, its metabolism. Thinking of a human-designed system as analogous to a natural system is a radical new idea. It is critical in a world where our decisions about the form and shape, or *morphology,* of human-designed objects and systems has profound consequences for the living systems in which they are embedded.

Design that learns from nature's examples is design that provides hope for the future and satisfaction in the present. Nature is unfolding wholeness. Nature lives by creating generative living structures that emerge and change through progressive transformations. They are never fixed. To transform design from mechanical processes and products requires a profound shift in how we understand design, nature, and ourselves.

Why has it taken so long for designers to discover the obvious and find ways to apply nature's lessons in design? The dualism that arose out of the early age of science and industrialism replaced the beauty and function of organic nature as the fountain of design inspiration with that of the machine—the tamer and dominator of untidy nature. The modernist movement in architecture heralded the rise of inexpensive mass technology as an equalizer and liberator of social and economic inequity. Modernism equated the clean, unadorned box and the straight, undecorated line with beauty and order. The reaction to these movements was Romanticism, which viewed nature as a Victorian-era virgin to be protected from defilement—again, a dualistic view that set nature apart and at the same time viewed her as passive rather than dynamic.

The overarching principle of sustainability is that of linked diversity. Within natural systems, it is the evolved diversity of species and niches that works to maintain stability in the face of big changes.

What nature does to combat instability in a particular environment is evolve an integrated or linked diversity in which many species at all scales are connected through flows and cycles. Rivers are designed to flood without doing harm. Their banks are lined with trees that prevent erosion. Their immediate low-lying areas or flood plains are populated with plants and animals that are adapted to thrive on occasional floods. Those places where two kinds of natural systems come together—for example, where forest meets grassland or where tidal waters meet land—are called ecotones, and they are typically places of maximum biological diversity and productivity. Although they are constantly changing, they maintain relative stability. Processes built on complex interlinked diversity are what sustainability is all about. We can apply the same criteria to guiding the future of our cities and regions.

Virtually everything we perceive as fixed is actually in a state of flow and change. Everything is engaged in an intricate dance that we can't see because the elements of the dance are either too large or too small, and the music being danced is either too fast or too slow for us to take notice.

Nature's design is adaptive design. Looking from the perspective of a very long time scale, design for adaptation equals evolution; at a short time scale, adaptation is ad hoc innovation and change. Ecologic design takes into account a wide time scale of adaptive strategies and scenarios integrating place, people, and pulse. Examples include changing landscapes and responses to global warming, the shift from command-and-control hierarchies to problem-solving networks, and the move from centralized energy sources to distributed sources such as fuel cells and rooftop photovoltaic panels.

the next leap forward: the integral age

> "The world is a fractal of ecologies, nested spheres of life, biospheres, and societies of mind. . . . The birth of a new consciousness seems to be part and parcel of the project to save the world." —S. J. Goerner, *After the Clockwork Universe*

Throughout this book I have been offering snapshots of the attributes of an architecture, a design process, and a culture and consciousness that are integral and ecological. The previous section presents many of the principles, processes, and ways of thinking that are the first wave of Integral design.

We are in the midst of a critical turning point as the dominant Mental consciousness unravels. Everywhere, centrally controlled command-and-control structures are being challenged by decentralized web-like structures. Belief in the material progress model based on science, technology, and unconstrained capitalism is being challenged in the developed and the developing world alike. Regional wars over increasingly scarce vital resources such as oil, water, and productive lands are increasing. Religious fundamentalism and endless wars of domination threaten stability and the specter of catastrophic ecologic collapse looms before us.

Integral	
Leap Forward	ASAP
Culture Form	Interconnected, interdependent webs
Space / Time Concept	Multi perspective / continuous present
Design Morphology	Eco-morphic
Prototype Geometry	Fractal
Prototype Built Form	Form follow flow; buildings as organism
Design Process	Collaborative, integrative, meta-discipline
Ecological Footprint	Integrated webs
Economics:	Distributed web, flow vs. accumulation, natural & human capitalism

In our present late state of Mental consciousness, the deficient forms of earlier cultural forms are at work. Extremist religious fundamentalism, an earlier Mythical form, is alive and well in the United States as well as in the Middle East, where the transition to Mental consciousness was never fully realized. Magical thinking is fed to us by television and other media. Five hundred channels of stories and events build our identification with cultural myths. We can stay young forever, even avoid death, if we buy the right products. We all can become rich, as indeed a majority of people in the United States believe they will. The wide emergence of forms of thought and action that represent long-repressed forms of earlier consciousness are signs of the breakdown of the existing dominant consciousness. Chaos and the emergence of the new are at work. As Thomas Berry tells us in *Dream of the Earth,* the world needs a new story to move into the Integral age.

turning point

What will be the turning point that will jump-start the great leap forward in global culture to an Integral worldview? Any transforming event grows out of the dynamics of chaotic change. It cannot be consciously willed. No one sat down to invent speech or agriculture. Indeed, they emerged at different places at the same time without a conscious plan. To restate Albert Einstein, "We cannot use the same thinking that created the problem to solve it."

The tragic events of September 11, 2001 (which have entered our culture collectively as the term 9/11) unleashed an accelerating and uncontrollable chaotic process of crisis and change. Some of the early response to 9/11 addressed the issue of fundamental change in our culture and consciousness. For a while, it seemed that this traumatic event might trigger a deep examination of our own culture and its direction. A November 11, 2001, op-ed piece in the *New York Times* had this to say: "Not knowing what to do with ourselves, we react to the unprecedented with the same old scripts—fly flags from car antennas, wear ribbons on our lapels—while wondering whether we should be aspiring higher, whether normal is really good enough anymore. We look everywhere for reassurance that the old life is returning. But simultaneously comes the vague yearning for some kind of fundamental change."

Bill Moyers, speaking to the Environmental Grant Makers Association on October 31, 2001, said, "We are at what educators call, 'a teachable moment.' And we'll lose if we roll over and shut up. What's at stake is democracy. . . . If you want to fight for the environment don't hug a tree, hug an economist. Hug the economist who tells you that fossil fuels are not only the third most heavily subsidized economic sector after road transportation and agriculture—they also promote vast inefficiencies. Hug the economist who tells you the most efficient investment of a dollar is not in fossil fuels but in renewable energy sources that not only provide new jobs but also cost less over time. . . . Do you want to send those terrorists a message? Go for clean, homegrown energy and go for public health."

Wendell Berry wrote on October 31, 2001, in a piece entitled "Thoughts in the Presence of Fear,"

"The time will soon come when we will not be able to remember the horrors of September 11 without remembering also the unquestioning technological and economic optimism that ended that day.

"The 'developed' nations have given to the 'free market' the status of a god, and were sacrificing to it their farmers, farmlands, and communities; their forests, wetlands and prairies, their ecosystems and watersheds. They had accepted universal pollution and global warming as normal costs of doing business.

"We had accepted too, the corollary belief that an economy (either as a money economy or life support system) that is global in extent, technologically complex, and centralized, is invulnerable to terrorism, sabotage, or war and that is protectable by 'national defense.'

"We can promote a decentralized world economy which would have the aim of assuring to every nation and region a local self-sufficiency in life-supporting goods. That would not eliminate international trade . . . ."

And speaking in November 2001 at a Sustainability Symposium at the University of Oklahoma, I had this to say: "Decisions that architects and engineers make and carry out for their clients account for half of our total energy and resource use. We know we can achieve the same or better quality results and reduce resource use to a quarter or a tenth of what we use now. It means moving from dumb design to smart design not only in buildings, but also land use planning, infrastructure design, and restoring natural systems to health.

"Today, America, with 4 percent of the world's population uses 40 percent of the world's resources. This is a violent, unnecessary, and unsustainable act. Every day, we are mindlessly destroying the harvest of four billion years of evolution. We are destroying life forms that can never be replaced, and risking the survival of our own species. When the going gets tough, it's the large mammals, including us, that are the first to die off. We are, as one of my mentors used to say, 'burning down the house of life in order to toast marshmallows.' We have set in motion a catastrophic holocaust of global warming, species extinction, air, water, and soil pollution—a world where every living system is under stress.

"You who are studying to be designers have a simple choice: you can lead a turn toward a sustainable world, or you can risk your life to preserve today's status quo. It's your choice to make: Will you be living in a green millennium or a brown and dying planet?"

In the short term, the events of 9/11 have been politically manipulated to breed fear and defensive disregard for the voices of change, propping up an already unraveling system for a last gasp. But everywhere, change is coming. Paul Hawken speaks of "a movement that has no name," the half-million global groups who, without shared ideology, are working to better the environments they live in. Connectivity is winning out over specialization. Environmentalism is teaching the world long-term thinking, in contrast to the dominant short-term time frames of governments and corporations. Hawken believes that the people of the planet are "developing a collective immune response" to the ideological response of the corporations and nation states. The severe consequences of climate change, when every place will change radically and we will not recognize home, may be the turning point that brings about a U-turn and leap forward.

A turning towards Integral consciousness centers on an awareness and direct experience of the interconnectedness, interdependence, and impermanence of all living systems, including each one of us. David Orr, in his book *Ecological Literacy,* writes that a deep understanding of how the natural environment works requires a merger of landscape and mindscape. "It is driven by a sense of wonder, the sheer delight in being alive in a beautiful, mysterious, bountiful world." We have all had these experiences from time to time. Imagine a life where we experience this feeling Orr describes every day!

cultural form

We can't predict the cultural forms that an Integral society might take, although there are clues in today's society. In a mobile, electronically connected society, community based on physical proximity is only one of many possibilities. While commuter suburbs of single-family homes have become the preferred living form in America for the last half century, there is much evidence to support the view that their design does not support community and people feel isolated.

The cultural form of the future will be web-like networks of people linked into a variety of subcultures based partially on traditional concepts of class, gender, age, religion and ethnicity, or employment. We already see whole other categories of community based on leisure activities, hobbies, and sports, lifestyles of health and sustainability, wellness, food preferences, and so on. Democracy requires active participation in the public business. Voting is not enough. Citizenship must be a daily practice, like going to the gym. The 2004 elections created a new web structure built through the Internet that gave people information not available in the mainstream media. The fractal-like Internet allowed people to begin to reclaim democracy.

There is a yearning for new forms of spatially defined communities that, through closely knit walkable neighborhoods, provide true variety and choice—convenience as well as active participation in creating and maintaining community. Cohousing is one such example, as is the renewal of many old urban neighborhoods. The key to Integral community is active participation, commitment, and the personal satisfaction that comes from being a part of a healthy and vibrant place.

integral space-time

Gebser's discussion of space-time suggests that for the Integral to come into being, transcending the Mental conceptions of three-dimensional space and linear time is essential. Seeing beyond the view of fixed perspective is a key in this transformation towards what I would call multi-perspectival consciousness. Gebser says, "The Integral is not a fusion of discrete material parts . . . which are always spatially bound."

Verition describes direct perception of what is true, without the filters and accoutrements of the rational mind. This is possible when the fixed point of the ego as the center of perception and thought is transcended. In other words, time-freedom, space–freedom, and ego-freedom all coincide. Aldous Huxley, in *The Doors of Perception*, makes a similar point: "Systematic reasoning is something we could not possibly do without. But neither . . . can we possibly do without direct perception . . . of the inner and outer worlds into which we have been born." Philosopher Huston Smith said, "Education is not the accumulation of information; it is the discovery of essential truth."

I have suggested that in ecological architecture, "Form follows flow." Stewart Brand expands on this theme in his book *How Buildings Learn*. Buildings are layered by different rates of change in the life of their essential components: site, structure, systems, skin, and fixtures and furnishings. By creating different use scenarios, we can design buildings that invite adaptation over time, rather than resist it.

Brand provides a framework that recasts time and space conceptions as the key dynamics of buildings that live and learn over time, and therefore are loved and last. He writes that the term, "'architecture' always means 'unchanging deep structure.' It is an illusion." He quotes British artist Brian Eno: "I think that humans have a taste for things that not only show they have been through a process of evolution, but which also show they are part of one."

The concept of the continuous present suggests that we and everything in our environment is in a continuous state of change. I have always resisted the accepted professional presumption that we must design everything down to the last detail on paper or in the computer before we build. I prefer to develop designs on-site and in construction, to work with clients and craftspeople to make changes as we go. Buildings seem to us as permanent, but buildings are always changing, never finished, always being and becoming.

integral morphology, geometry, and built form

Integral design creates buildings and environments that are "ecomorphic;" that is, their internal structure mimics and integrates with the natural systems within which they are embedded and connected. Ecomorphism means something different than an architectural form derived directly from nature, such as the structure of a bridge resembling the structure of a bird wing, or a house looking like a nautilus shell. These are examples of biomorphism, forms taken directly from nature. Ecomorphism goes deeper, implying architectural processes and forms at many scales adapted to nature.

An ecological approach to design follows a very simple observation: Architecture is a dynamic adaptation to place, people, and pulse. This simple dictum proposes that architecture respond to these key shapers of form. Most contemporary buildings are shaped by the abstract short-run economic programs of corporate and institutional clients and by the fashion dictates of their architects. People, the eventual users and occupants of a building, enter most building programs only as a quantitative factor, not as a qualitative cocreator, inhabitant, and change agent of built form. Short-run, narrow-focus economics dominates the design program and design process.

Buildings are not fixed entities. They are like other organisms, constantly changing due to the throughput of energy, materials, information, and context. The reason that buildings exist is people. Stewart Brand suggests that people will always find a way to change buildings that their designers thought of as fixed and immutable. An ecologic design process invites "nonprofessionals," the building's users and occupants, to be active participants in the design process. An ecologic building is designed to adapt to changing human needs, wants, preferences, and aversions.

Integrally designed communities and cities will be conceived as ecosystems that integrate natural and designed systems at similar scale levels as discussed in the last section. For example, rainwater runoff from streets and roofs is not shoved in a pipe and sent elsewhere but instead is retained on-site through cisterns, absorptive surfaces, or local retention ponds. Rather than being piped in from afar, energy is produced locally through rooftop solar devices, and carbon dioxide is absorbed by trees, green roofs, and green walls. Fractal forms become part of the urban pattern.

Another aspect of Integral built form is that its physical character and form are biophilial. The famed naturalist E. O. Wilson first articulated the concept and the term as "the innately emotional affiliation of human beings to other living organisms. Innate means hereditary and hence part of human nature." Our sense of beauty is hard-wired into us through our million years of living in nature. In the Integral epoch, we will again recognize that the source for all beauty is the natural world.

Previously, I've discussed the classes of patterns that make up the living world. Only the crystalline lattice pattern contains the grid-like cube that is the monomorphic, monotonous form that engulfs our everyday environment, creating the experience of living in a sterile geography of nowhere. If the lattice and the cube are the prototypical geometry of today's rational-mental world, then the self-similarity of the fractal will be the prototypical geometry of the Integral Era. However far you zoom in or out of a fractal system, there will always be an unending cascade of self-similar but not identical detail. It is interesting to note that other classes of natural patterns may also exhibit the fractal property of self-similarity: spirals, meanders, branching, waves, symmetry, and nets.

The discovery of fractals as a distinct class of patterns stemming from seemingly chaotic behavior was first discovered by the French mathematician Benoit Mandelbrot. Plotting the geometry of seemingly chaotic number series, he discovered that they generated a beautiful fractal configuration. An occurrence that mechanistic science wrote off as disorder and chaos turns out to be a higher, more complex level of order that is now used to describe phenomenon as diverse as the behavior of the stock market, the activity of our brains and hearts, and weather systems. Chaos represents higher order levels of dynamic change and cooperation.

James Gleick, in his landmark book, *Chaos: Making a New Science,* describes the emotional parallels between the new mathematical esthetic discovered by chaos theorists and art and architecture: "To Mandelbrot and his followers . . . simple shapes are inhuman. They fail to resonate with the way nature organizes itself or with the way human perception sees the world. . . . Why is it that the silhouette of a storm-bent leafless tree against an evening sky in winter is perceived as beautiful, but the corresponding silhouette of any multi-purpose university building is not, in spite of any efforts of the architect? . . . Our feeling for beauty is inspired by the harmonious arrangement of order and disorder as it occurs in natural objects."

The prototypical built form of the Integral world is the open, integrative, dynamic network in which the flows of the living world and the designed world are intricately linked together. Notice how in the integral ring diagram, nature, design, and culture are all integrally interconnected without sharp boundaries.

Cities and towns that grew organically over time in preindustrial times have many of the characteristics of fractals in that they build from a repertoire of complex similar parts, common details, shapes, materials, and levels of scale. The fractal is the prototypical built form of Integrality. I can imagine neighborhoods whose buildings and systems are built fractal-like, each piece part of an emerging whole pattern. Combined with ecomorphism, where the lines between what is nature and what is man-made are blurred, the concept becomes obvious. Green roofs that mirror the topography of the surrounding hills are one such example.

At the land planning and infrastructure scale, using fractal patterns minimizes the disruption of the already-existing fractal patterns. Tim Duane, a University of California planner, discovered that the best way to plan wildlife corridors in rural areas with conventional subdivisions was to create an intricate fractal pattern of open space. Engineers designing to control flooding are abandoning the heavy-handed, straight concrete banks in favor of fractal-like, absorbent marsh flood zones as a more effective, economical, and esthetic solution.

The geometry of the individual building won't develop fractal forms until the design process recognizes that buildings can't be designed as completed, unchanging entities. The whole idea of the single, isolated building is antithetical to Integral thinking. New design and production technology in the building products industry suggests that a move from standard linear and planar components to more intricate configurations is possible. The literal "greening" of buildings through layering vertical walls of living plants as an outer wall in front of our glass-clad cities as well as greening the roofs, could bring the fractal scale of nature to every urban high-rise occupant and provide a carbon dioxide sink in cities where we need it most.

design processes

Integral culture and Integral design processes are closely linked. Living in an Integral world of body/mind, nature, and built environment, we experience all of life as an interconnected, self-organizing, coevolving whole. The shift from self to self-organizing webs serving a larger common good brings into being new cultural patterns reflected in all key institutional forms and processes, including built form at all scales.

Integral culture's features include social, economic, and physical forms and processes that are

- Intricate, adaptable networks rather than command-and-control dominator hierarchies.
- Collaborative, flexible, and creative design processes. The design team is metadisciplinary, composed of people whose specialized expertise fits into a shared Integral framework, language, and worldview.
- The focus of self-interest is modulated by mutual interests as society becomes engaged in a cooperative effort to rebuild a living world and a revitalized community.
- The flow of information in computer networks linked planet-wide that cannot be easily controlled and managed by hierarchical organizations. Intelligence is distributed throughout societies. The equity of distributed intelligence begins to transform the social and economic inequities of a global economy that currently funnels money, power, and resources to a few nations
- Today, globalization controlled by a small number of powerful organizations is creating a monocultural world. Integral design processes supported by decentralized webs of information create diversity and unity simultaneously. A fractal world creates fractal forms.

ecologic footprint

The consequences of a shift to the Integral Age will be a vastly reduced ecological footprint in the developed nations combined with a more equitable sharing of resources with the majority of people who live on the planet. A global program for regenerating degraded ecosystems is essential. In another fifty years, fossil fuels will no longer be an option to provide the energy to run buildings, transport, industry, and agriculture. Solar, wind, hydrogen, and biomass will replace oil and gas, together with vastly improved efficiency. Zero waste, 100 percent recycling and remanufacture will be the norm. We will be designing smarter by a factor of ten.

economics

Remember that the words "economy" and "ecology" come from the same Greek word, *oikos,* or house. Ecology refers to the logic of our shared house, Earth. Economy refers to the nomia—quantification or management of our Earth household. The natural capital concept attempts to bridge the current disconnect between the two. It is an important first step. Theoretically, corporations that made the connection would win out in a resource-scarce polluted world, but such ethical thinking is just in the first stages of entering the corporate world.

In the next decades, the world will be struggling with the impacts of global warming. The fossil fuel era is ending. Great challenges lie ahead.

This leap forward is possible. With the survival of our planet and its rich variety of inhabitants at stake, new ideas and technologies will emerge to help usher in a new integral world.

EPILOGUE

Fountain at Highland House Inverness.

My continuing journey in designing for life is an ever-changing web of many converging interconnections and interdependencies. I wrote many years ago, "I try to find the root; finding the root is the route." The route has many branches that formed me, inform my work, and continually enrich my life—an ecology of family, friends, colleagues, mentors, and places. This epilogue is a grateful reflection on, and acknowledgement of, my companions along the route we've shared.

The Lindisfarne Association, Esalen Institute, and San Francisco Zen Center, all created in the 1960s, became the communities that nourished my mind and heart, helped shape the sensibility that guides my work, and also gave me unique opportunities to design and build for them. The leaders of these three special learning communities—Bill Thompson of Lindisfarne, Michael Murphy of Esalen, and Richard Baker of San Francisco Zen Centers—are like conductors who wrote their own music, developed their own instruments, and recruited talented musicians to perform a new kind of music.

Cultural historian William Irwin Thompson founded the Lindisfarne Association to create together a fellowship of individuals whose work focused on the ideas and tools necessary to build a post-mechanical, post-dualism society. Bill had written a popular book in 1971. *At the Edge of History* made the case that we were entering a new era that unified science, spirit, ecology, and technology into a new type of society, community, and personhood. He included stories of his encounters with then-new types of centers such as Esalen. First in New York and then later in a new center in Crestone, Colorado, which I designed, Bill brought together an ever-expanding group of the Fellows for a week of presentations, discussions, and bull sessions around particular themes that Bill framed in his opening remarks, which themselves were remarkable as rapid fire, lyric, soaring, no-notes performances.

I was invited to join in 1976 and for the next twenty years hungrily fed my mind and spirit at the annual Lindisfarne event, where I met and interacted with the people who helped shape and inspire a new sensibility. Some I already knew individually. The magic was the chemistry that came out of the week, of conversation with Fellows including poet Gary Snyder, agriculturalist Wes Jackson, farmer/writer Wendell Berry, bioneers John and Nancy Todd, anthropologist Mary Catherine Bateson, biologist Stuart Kaufman, economist Hazel Henderson, anthropologist Gregory Bateson, artist Mayumi Oda, Esalen founder Michael Murphy, economist Brian Arthur, botanist Gary Nabhan, educator David Orr, Richard Baker, Abbott of Zen Center, banker Michaela Walsh, energy guru Amory Lovins, nonprofit organizer and author L. Hunter Lovins, author and entrepreneur Paul Hawken, founder of the Whole Earth Catalog Stewart Brand, mathematician Ralph Abraham, musician Paul Winter, and architect Paolo Soleri. I'm grateful to all of them.

zen center

I got to know Richard Baker shortly after the San Francisco Zen Center acquired Tassajara, a hot spring retreat deep in the mountains behind Big Sur. Not too long after that he was made Abbott of Zen Center by its founder and spiritual leader, Suzuki Roshi. Baker Roshi has an amazing network of friends in the arts, business, entertainment, politics, philosophy, and religion.

He has a deep interest and knowledge in all the arts and architecture. Under his leadership, Zen Center undertook a major expansion in both accommodations for students and their practice, and also Zen Center-related enterprises that could provide needed income and employment.

He invited me to work on Zen Center's projects. George Wheelwright, the coinventor of Polaroid, gifted Green Gulch ranch on the California Coast to Zen Center. I worked with Richard on a plan to add meeting and guest facilities and connect them to an expanded ranch house that included dining and kitchen facilities. From there we went on to Tassajara and the design of a courtyard complex of guest rooms close to the creek. Later came the Guest House and another solar residence at Green Gulch and Greens Restaurant in 1979. I was happy to work for no fee. Richard's combination of clarity, trust, and steadfast commitment to quality set the bar for me in selecting future clients. That, combined with a master builder crew led by Paul Discoe, who would take my concept drawings and translate them into reality without the usual ego war between architect and builder, made working for Zen Center always a pleasure.

The buildings follow the traditional Japanese style, which has always attracted me. Our most recent project built in the early 1990s is the meditation hall or *zendo* for his new center in Colorado. We did the basic design over a weekend in Inverness. The building is simple and follows the golden mean proportions. The shell was built by a local barn builder and the beautiful traditional interiors were created by Len Brackett, a skilled Japanese-trained carpenter.

esalen

At Michael Murphy's seventieth birthday party on a yacht in San Francisco Bay, I made a banner that said, "Happy Birthday to the Irish Pirate of the Soul." Through his energy, enthusiasm, insight, and intellect, Michael has created a series of revolutions in world culture, including cofounding Esalen with Dick Price as a place devoted to the study and expansion of human potential. In Michael's world, this includes mind, body, and spirit as a unified whole. He has been at the forefront of work in all three areas. I first met him through Dr. Frank Barron, a renowned psychologist. Michael invited us to go down to Esalen, where over the year I attended a variety of workshops. Later he asked me to develop a master plan and design for new facilities. Michael was always open to my workshops, where I tested out my latest ideas on the diverse students Esalen attracted. Michael is an amazing combination of monk, scholar, cultural innovator, and author. He and his work continue to inspire me.

colleagues and collaborators in design

Among architects, gentleness is not common. Coming to teach at Berkeley, I was greeted and guided by a gifted and gentle man, Charles Moore. With his immense curiosity, erudition, and dry humor, he believed that design education should be an open dialogue among people of diverse ideas and passions. The school prospered under his quiet leadership, which encouraged not ideology but open exploration of ideas.

Among the newcomers was Christopher Alexander, with whom I taught and argued for many years. Chris was always intense and seldom gentle—a tireless explorer of a new terrain, mapping the underlying structures he saw as the true generators of form. In writing this book, I have been reading his opus, *The Nature of Order*, and realize how much our paths have overlapped and how his insights seeped into my own understanding.

Sandy Hirshen, my high school classmate, architectural partner, and lifelong friend is a gentle, compelling person who has steadfastly translated the ethic of social justice into an architecture for all the people.

Jim Campe has been a model of steadfastness to principles and devotion to family, friends, community, and clients. He never separates his work as an architect from the rest of his life.

Peter Calthorpe is a prodigious thinker and doer. I met him when he was in his early twenties, brought him to Farallones, and later asked him to join me in Sacramento. We were partners after that for some years and together developed many of the principles and examples that form the basis for today's sustainable development movement.

When I formed Van der Ryn Architects and the Ecological Design Institute in 1995, I was fortunate to attract an extremely diverse and gifted team of collaborators. I offer thanks especially to Pete Retondo, Marci Riseman, David Arkin, Rebecca Coffman, Dierdre Holmes, Andrea Traber, Rob Pena, Dave Deppen, Buddy Williams, So Young Mack, Kathleen Smith, Noel Manarud, Chris Gutsche, Kim Sarnecki, Michael Heacock, Alex Von Deling, Rose Singles, and all the rest of our team over the past ten years.

family

My family is the anchor that has secured me from drifting away in many a storm. My mother's gift to me was her spirit. Born into a strict Dutch Jewish family, she was rebellious and free-spirited, but there was not much support for that sort of a young woman growing up in those times. She married my father when she was twenty-one. Ten years and three children later, we immigrated to New York on the eve of the Nazi invasion of Poland. Holland soon fell as well and we lost contact with our extended family, all of whom chose to remain in Holland. Few survived that Holocaust.

In 1946, my mother returned to Holland to find her brother's children who were separated from their parents when they were transported to death camps and had survived. Heleen, six at the time, joined our family and I became an older brother to her, involving her in my love of animals and the outdoor life. She married her high school sweetheart, and moved to New Hampshire, where

OPPOSING PAGE
Fountain and Pond in Highland garden.

they have lived for many years. She overcame her own learning disabilities, and became a professor of Special Education, tirelessly and empathetically working with children's learning problems. She and my mother were especially close and devoted to each other. Now retired, Heleen is active in her local community and was recently elected Selectwoman.

My mother and I had an often-turbulent relationship. She would oscillate between expressing fury at my undisciplined nature and then becoming a partner in my adventures. I shared a small bedroom with my orderly, science-minded older brother. Critters I had found in vacant lots freely roamed the room, like garter snakes and things that I found for them to eat. I started raising hamsters, whose gnawing drove my brother to threaten me with a kitchen knife while I cowered outside on the ledge of the fourth-story window. The next day while I was at school, Mother threw out all the assorted living detritus I had collected in vacant lots and marshlands, which had filled the room. I came home, viewed the sterile, vacant space and yelled, "You have just killed my world!" She consulted a psychiatrist, who told her I was right. She threatened to send me to military school. The next day she got up early to buy special goodies for my lunch.

Some of our best times were trips we took together when I was a teenager to our favorite sanctuary, the remote Long Island beaches. She cherished my drawings, watercolors, and objects I made out of driftwood.

My father's family had a nonferrous manufacturing and distribution business founded by my great-great grandfather. From my mother's stories, I was left with the impression that he was expected to enter the business. When we fled to this country, my father joined the government-in-exile business offices located in New York. He was a gentle person but emotionally distant, and seemed distracted with business and family worries. When he was home, he spent hours in his den with his stamp collections and crossword puzzles. I longed for a hug or his attention. He seldom had much to say to me except to ask about my grades. After the war, he debated returning to Holland but opted to set up a successful business importing and distributing copper and brass products from European mills. He retired from business at sixty. He died in 1980 after some years of being afflicted with Alzheimer's disease. Our relationship was never completed. He is often in my dreams as the father I wish he'd been.

For the next seventeen years my mother lived alone in the house, taking more opportunities to exercise her inner spirit. She babysat and nurtured twin girls for years. She went folk dancing every week, volunteered at the hospital, and made friends everywhere she went. She was self-sufficient until her death at age ninety. During her last weeks, I was in Italy in daily touch by phone. Not many words were spoken, but I knew that she identified with my journey and took pleasure in the person I had become.

My siblings, brother Jack and sister Fredericka, are five and six years older than me, an age difference that separated us during the early years of our exodus to America. In adulthood, that changed, especially with my brother. After a long and distinguished career in the federal government, his passion increasingly turned towards the environment. After retiring from federal service, he became the environmental officer of a Washington-based foundation, a much-respected elder in environmentally based philanthropy. Increasingly, our interests have merged, with each of us using our different skills to advance a more equitable, ecological world. My sister, after raising five children in the fifties, continues to lead an active and full life.

I married Mimi when I was twenty, and we were both in school in Ann Arbor. Fifty years later we are friends although we divorced thirty years ago. We soon had three children and a big

FACING
Sim circa 1974 in Highland House. Photography by Art Rogers.

house in the Berkeley Hills, and I was an up-and-coming professor with an already-impressive resume.

She held the family together through her nurturing presence, her great cooking and baking, and her love for our children and for me. She is a bright, warm, presence. Mimi now has her own practice as a family therapist in northern California.

We moved to the country in 1969 after the People's Park episode. We filled the space with a constant stream of interesting people, spontaneous parties, a ritual Friday-night wood sauna for the community, Saturday volleyball on the beach, and wild celebrations on the solstices and equinoxes.

In 1974–75, I was engaged in setting up our institute in Occidental. I went to an open house at Julie's high school and met her weaving teacher, Ruth. We began seeing each other.

By the end of that summer, it was clear I was going to Sacramento to join the Brown administration. I asked Ruth to join me.

That was thirty years ago and we have passed through many lives, weaving our two different, strong personalities together. From being a talented weaver, Ruth has become a successful designer and businesswoman manufacturing her highly regarded fabric to the interior furnishing market. She works in a refurbished waterfront studio a half mile from our houseboat home.

I have learned through our years together that it's possible to have a committed, loving, relationship based on companionship, common interests, and shared values without compromising our need to each fully develop and live out our own vision and life.

My children have enormously enriched my life through their own unique personalities and the life journeys they share with me.

Julie went to college for a year, worked in San Francisco, Europe, and New York, where she met Dario, a warmhearted, talented Italian designer. They married, had their first child, Damiano, and then moved to Madrid, where Luna was born. About ten years ago they moved back to California and now live in Napa. Five years ago, Julie enrolled in an accelerated bachelor's and master's program. She now teaches in a local university and coordinates their service learning program. Damiano is now fourteen, and Luna twelve. To experience the close-knit, openly loving quality of their family is always a delight for me, as is Julie's new career and exceptional ability to frame complex philosophic issues in a personal context.

After receiving a degree in Ecological Studies from UC Santa Cruz, and a master's degree in Ethnographic Film and Anthropology from the University of Southern California, Micah moved to Samoa. There he teaches in a community college. He is married to a wonderful Samoan woman and they have three beautiful children. He's made a number of documentaries on the tension between traditional and modern cultures in Samoa and is writing a book on the influence of Western culture on traditional Samoan architecture and community.

Over the past twenty years, Ethan has developed his career as a highly regarded film sound editor and designer on major movies, culminating in receiving the Academy Award in 2003 as supervising sound editor for *Lord of the Rings: Two Towers.* Since 1988, he has been credited for his work on more than thirty major films.

home and the continuous present

Few people are able to design and build their own home and live in it for most of their lives. The experience has been one of the biggest teachers in my life. Our home has been a continuous work in progress for more than thirty years. The environment surrounding it has lived through years of drought, a major flood, and a forest fire that came so close we prepared to say good-bye.

A friend remarked that most houses are museums to one's past. Creating the form and physical container for one's own life is a deep, satisfying, and sometimes terrifying experience. Most of the designer/owner/builders I know had to let go of most of the fixed images they developed over the years. The process of designing, building, and living in your own house reveals the connectedness of architecture to life. In spite of my career in teaching and practicing design, it exposed my deep ignorance of many practical matters.

The rhythms of nature are like a human pulse, punctuated by surge events that result in dramatic changes in the local ecology. You learn to read the mood and flavor of weather changes, native animals, and plants. Fecundity and growth go hand in hand with decay and death in a continuing cycle of regeneration.

In earlier chapters, I've mentioned several of the homes I built for my family after moving from Berkeley to the California coast. The first house, constructed around the cabin I'd built some years earlier using the panel system Sandy Hirshen and I developed for the Migrant Housing Program, never felt right to me. Soon after finishing it, I bought a secluded five-acre parcel high on a ridge surrounded by permanent open space. This is the setting for *Making a Place in the Country* in 1971. The site had a 1950s cabin on it. In 1972, I started adding onto the cabin with a pole-barn-type structure that is still home and still evolving. Its name is Highland House.

The design of Highland House used construction techniques inspired by two architect friends: Igor Sazevich, a neighbor in Inverness, and Peter Sellers, in Warren, Vermont. Instead of building with frame walls and floors, Igor had designed some homes using a pole barn technique: twelve inch-diameter poles planted six feet into the ground as vertical supports, horizontal beams to create the frame, and then walls and floors of solid, three-inch cedar that were the finished interior and exterior.

I had visited David Sellers in Vermont, where he was building a number of innovative structures using salvage materials. He had bought large rolls of clear acrylic "seconds," which he used profusely instead of windows. I bought a two-thousand-square-foot roll of the material from Los Angeles and used it extensively to build a clear roof and long half-cylinder windows. I spent about a year building the three-story addition with the help of two students who had participated in *Making a Place in the Country*. In addition to these basic materials, we used windows salvaged in Berkeley.

The house had been built fifteen feet away from the existing cabin. When we had it enclosed, we tackled the problem of how to connect the two structures. Tom McCoy, an experienced carpenter who had also been in the 1971 course, drew a quick sketch of a pyramidal roof held up by a long twelve-by-twelve redwood beam we'd salvaged in Mendocino along with a beautiful redwood water tank, which later became the sauna.

In 1978, I returned to Highland House with Ruth. With her designer's eye, she made a number of changes. The Plexiglas went. Ruth designed cherry cabinets that a local cabinetmaker built to replace my own crude chain-sawed cedar cabinets. A Farallones craftsman replaced the ladder that went up to what had been the kids' loft with a beautiful spiral staircase built around an old utility pole, adding reclaimed fir steps and a railing built of salvaged redwood tank staves.

Ruth also expanded our rudimentary garden, clearing away the brush that came right up to the house. In 1983, we rented Highland House and moved to Sausalito. Most of our spare time was engaged in Farallones, where we undertook necessary upgrades. In 1990, the Farallones Rural Center was sold to another nonprofit organization.

We plunged into a new round of construction at Highland House. We tore down the original plywood cabin, leaving only the floor. Ken Sawyer, the head carpenter at Zen Center with whom I'd worked, camped out with his son Micah for six months and built the Japanese-style pavilion we'd designed to replace the cabin. The thousand-square-foot room incorporated kitchen, dining, and living space. Ken and Micah built everything on-site using Japanese joinery. The result was a simple, airy, beautiful space. We also set to work remodeling the original pole barn, adding bathrooms and improving the main great room.

The renewed Japanese wing seemed to call for an outdoor space that matched its simplicity and craftsmanship. Slowly, we were pushing back the bishop pine forest and brush, which crowded the building, robbed light, and presented a fire and falling hazard. We worked with Lance Wyeth, a local designer/builder, to build stone walls, a large flagstone patio, and several water elements (which I am fond of designing and experiencing).

In October 1995, a major forest fire broke out on the mountaintop above us. The winds swept it south to the ridge where I'd built our first house and designed many others. Sixty houses were destroyed, the winds shifted, and our neighboring six-hundred-acre Nature Conservancy Bishop Pine Preserve went up in flames. The Inverness Ridge fire was being fought by several thousand firefighters, assisted by helicopters and borate bombers. It had burned thousands of acres of grassland and forest in Point Reyes National Seashore.

A company of firefighters assigned to protect property was camped out on our new bocce ball court and terrace. The fire line was a quarter mile away at the neighbors. The fire captain assigned to protect our home advised us to remove what we wanted to save from the house and get ready to leave.

We filled up two pickups and waited, running up to the fire front to check on how things looked. Eight helicopters carrying three-thousand-gallon buckets made the five-minute trip from the bay to the ridge fire from dawn till dusk. Never had the sound of helicopters sounded like music to our ears. They stopped the fire at our neighbors' property.

The fire brought big changes. The surviving bishop pines were attacked by beetles, and we had to remove a number that threatened to fall on the house. We cleared a larger garden space, bringing in much more light. Ten years later, walking through the burn area is a reassuring experience in nature's power of regeneration. The new bishop pines are thick and twenty feet tall.

We're still always busy with new projects at Highland House. It's an ever-evolving landscape of change, connectivity, and impermanence. Some say that architecture is a manifestation of our denial of death, the desire to create things that live beyond us. Yes, our buildings often do outlive us, but not without constant vigilance and care. Landscapes have

OPPOSITE
Clockwise, starting with top left: Highland House around 1972; replacing the original cabin in 1990; Highland House today.

RIGHT
Looking up into the pyramidal entry hall.

OPPOSITE
Clockwise, starting with top left: kitchen; entry hall; entry; living room in main wing.

nature's mind. We attend their growth and change as we would tend a child. Maybe a dream is to make our houses more like living landscapes, with minds of their own.

Lastly, I want to thank special friends whose advice and encouragement have been of enormous help: Paul and Charlene Lee, Elizabeth Garsonin, Marty and Pamela Krasney, Bob Twiss and Amy Skewes Cox, Susan Hughes, Tony Kline and Sharon Jones, Randy Hayes and Lauren Klein Hayes, David Isis Schwartz, Jonathan and Diana Rose, David and Sara Gottfried, David Harris, Cherie Forrester, Virginia Baker, Rene Des Tombes, Diana Cohn, Steve and Kay McNamara, Bill and Carol Press, David and Suzanne Warner, Jeff Steen and Paul Frankel, Gigi Sims, John and Maddie Francis, and Jim and Pam Campe.

Writing and producing this book has been its own journey. I wouldn't have begun without the help of Kim Cross, a gifted young journalist who coached me through the first chapters. My assistants, Kim Sarnecki and Olivier Pennetier, kept me and the work organized over the last five years.

I knew the right publisher would appear at the right time. Thank you, Gibbs Smith, for your support and faith in me. Your beautiful and thought-provoking books stand out. The team—including editor Buckley Jeppson, managing editor Madge Baird, art director Kurt Wahlner, and designer Tom Sieu—offered valuable advice and insight at every step along the editing and production process to bring this book to you.

FAR LEFT
Interior nook

LEFT, TOP
Highland House bathroom

LEFT, BOTTOM
Highland House bedroom

index

photo credits

Jess Alford: 139 bottom left
Richard Barnes: 58, 76, 77 top and bottom, 78, 80, 81
Charles C. Benton: front jacket, 2, 79, 153 top right
Warren Bolster: 148 bottom center
Gerry Campbell: 140 bottom left
Comstock Images: 136 top left, 148 top center
Donald Corner: 65
Adam Crowley: 139 top left
Russ Eddy: 82 top, 86
Fotocea Storica Nazional: 140 top left
Tom Fox: 140 top right
Joshua Freiwald: 20, 28, 29 top right, 36 right, 38
Geostock: 136 bottom left
David Hoptman: 100, 111
James Hubbell: 112 top and bottom, 113 bottom
Hisham F. Ibrahim: 139 bottom right
InterNetwork Media: 148 bottom left
Cathy Kelly: 64
Stuart Lirette: 160, 173 top right, 174 top right
C. Ray Moore: 2
Jon Naar: 107
Olivier Pennetier: 148 top left, top second from left, bottom second from left
Photo 24: 136 top right
PhotoDisc Collection: 139 top right
Red Horse Constructors: 87, top and center right
Art Rogers: 61, 166
Roofscapes, Inc.: 118 left and right, 119
Robert Shlatter: back jacket flap
Stockbyte: 140 bottom right
Suzan Storch: 171 top right and bottom, 172, 173 top left, center and bottom, 174 bottom right
Jeremy Woodhouse: 135
Peter Xiques: 70 top